Front cover photograph is of the Fairchild children. Top to bottom: Thomas-6, Ella "Teena"-4 and Nelda "Sunny"-3.

Sing or Cry

My Life in Verse

Poems

by

Sunny Bingo

Nelda "Sunny" Bingo

a.k.a. Ned Fairchild

First Edition

2006

ASPEN'D PUBLISHING

ASHTON, IDAHO

Sing or Cry
My Life in Verse

ISBN 978-09748515-3-2
Library of Congress Control Number: 2006928971

Bingo, Nelda.
Sing or Cry : my life in verse : poems / by Nelda "Sunny" Bingo, a.k.a. Ned Fairchild. -- 1st ed.
p. cm.
LCCN 2006928971
ISBN 978-09748515-3-2
ISBN 0-9748515-3-1

I. Title.

PS3602.I547S56 2006 811'.6
QBI06-600263

Book design by Chan Atchley
Cover design and graphic enhancements of original pen and pencil sketches by Judith Atchley
Printed in Canada by Friesens Book Division
Published by Aspen'd Publishing
Box 855
Ashton, Idaho 83420

09-2006

Table of Contents

Sing or Cry

To Evelyn and Thomas
whose sibling love surely saved my life,
and especially to my confidant, sister and buddy Teena
who has been a constant inspiration.
And last, but not least,
to my life's companion Richard "Bing" Bingo
and my talented, loving children.

About the Author

Nelda "Sunny" Bingo
June 2006

Few of us can truly appreciate the trauma of being born cross-eyed in a time when there was no surgical remedy. Combine that with being so poor that going to bed hungry was a common occurrence and then to suffer through the taunting and often physical abuse of other children because of her "devil eyes," and one has to wonder how Nelda "Sunny" Fairchild Bingo born August 16, 1929 in Burley, Idaho could have possibly grown up to be "normal." Add to that the trauma of a family constantly on the move as her stepfather went from one "hot rivet" job to another and another.

By her count, Sunny attended at least 30 different grammar schools. One can only imagine the trauma she endured each time this cross-eyed little girl changed schools. When nine years old she was nearly killed when struck by a car. She sustained a fractured skull and broken collar bone.

Sunny literally attributes her survival to singing. It was the only way to vent her frustrations and be her own person. When things were at their worst, instead of wallowing in self pity she, like her other siblings, sang! It was also how they earned money to feed and clothe the family.

As a singer, she also became a song writer under the pseudonym of "Ned Fairchild." Among her creations, the most notable hit was *Twenty Flight Rock* recorded by Eddy Cochrane that ushered in the Rock and Roll era. Many of her songs were recorded and made famous by other great artists such as Gene Autry, Mick Jagger, Paul McCartney, and Merle Travis.

A consummate writer, Sunny also penned poems expressing her many experiences and thoughts in verse. Some experiences however, were simply too painful and emotional to recount in verse. There are few poems about her childhood and adolescent years. There is no mention of her first marriage at age 15 in 1944 to Jack Farnsworth who fought in the South Pacific during World War II, was disabled by malaria, and came home a war hero. Nor has she written anything about the divorce that left her a single mother of a four-year-old son.

She wrote many songs while married to Richard "Bing" Bingo, whom she met and married in 1950. Together they had two children, Jill and Frank, and Sunny's song writing and poetry proliferated. But, as her poems will attest, these were also troubling times. She was often on the road selling her songs and doing "gigs," singing in bars and lounges with a small band.

After Bing's death from cancer in 1992, Sunny bought a local "watering hole" in Ashton, Idaho, ran it for three years, then sold it for a nice profit and retired. During the next three years she and her sister Teena often sang together at benefits, and as "casual" singers with local musicians in motel lounges and for special events.

In 2000, Sunny moved to Seattle so she could be closer to her son Frank. Then, with the death of her sister Teena's husband, Sunny moved back to Ashton where she now resides. They occasionally sing at special events and Sunny has been busy with the publication of this book.

"I hope readers of this book," she says, "will find what I have written helpful while confronting their own problems. Sometimes it helps just to know that someone has been through what you are going through.

"The reason I wrote the book," she continues, "is summarized in the following poem."

Unburdened Heart

Though none call me poet when I am gone,
Someone may find this little book and read
How I was battered blue and left to bleed
Insensible, on life's threshing stone.
Not just for my sake or soul's own purging,
Do I march these words across the page;
Perhaps old sentiments mossed green with age
Can comfort some far heart with sorrow
burgeoning.
If another weep in sweet release
Of pent up griefs that overwhelm them so.
Cries across the years, "I know, I know!
Your pain is mine." This somehow gives me peace;
A narrow respite from the constancy
Of anguish that did not begin with me.

To Chan and Judith
whose invaluable guidance and counsel
made this book possible,
Thank You!

About the Book

Rarely does one have the privilege of publishing something truly unique. We have been twice blessed. To get to know an individual who has, in the jargon of the West, "been up the river and over the mountain of life" is indeed a very rare event. Then, to get the opportunity to publish a collection of poems so compelling and different is one of those memorable experiences of a lifetime.

Another unique feature of this book of poems is the graphics that go with it. There are more than 100 original pen and ink illustrations drawn by the author as she wrote the poems. They are connected in some way to the verse and help convey the feelings she experienced as she wrote them.

In an effort to capture the emotion of the verse and tell a story, the verses are organized more or less in chronological order and structured very much like that of a novel. Thoughtfully looking into the meaning of each verse provides insight into the torment of a very courageous and creative person making her way through life.

The book contains five chapters and five parts. Each chapter and part has a title page with a verse that characterizes its contents. The first chapter contains poems written about the author's challenged childhood. The second chapter is about an almost idyllic life in California and the trauma of losing her first love to World War II.

Chapter III is a collection of poems titled "Marriage" and loosely divided into five "Parts." Poems found in each of the five parts are loosely arranged in chronological order, but with a difference. These poems deal more with subject matter than with time. This is particularly important to keep in mind as you read the first five parts that deal with the raw emotion and consequences of living life to its fullest.

On the lighter side, Chapter IV is dedicated to a few fun verses that provide meaning to the occasional mischievous glint in the author's now healthy uncrossed eyes. Chapter V is about the trauma of dealing with life after the death of her husband.

We hope you enjoy reading this book of emotional poems as much as we did while getting them ready for publication.

Chapter I

Growing Up

I wanted only one
Star up in the sky
To make a wish upon.
I never asked to fly
To Star-studded worlds
Only one Star, one wish come true
For good little girls.

Sing or Cry

Children laughed, crossed their eyes,
Pointed fingers, pushed me, would shout,
"Cross-eyed monkey!" I didn't know why,
I was on the "inside" looking out.

Dear brother knew, my sisters too,
Numbers did not matter,
They did what loving siblings do,
Words and fists made my tormenters scatter.

Tears dried, my scraped knees healed,
Pity was not a word I heeded,
Music and prose became my saving grace,
It gave my soul a secret place.

When four and five, hunger held us hostage,
We sang in harmony, a bar room floor our stage,
Mother picked up coins that came our way,
There would be food for another day.

Bundled in a patch work quilt,
While Mother kneaded dough for bread.
The light from an old oil lamp,
Cast shadows on the bed.

Putting kids to bed with nothing to eat,
Mother wished it wasn't so.
She turned away to hide her tears,
It broke her heart to tell us no.

Mother worked so very hard,
To keep us fed and dry.
Her love, so sweet, we savored,
Our choice was to sing or cry.

Self Portrait

Part child, part whim,
(Part memory of him)
Some music, some rhyme,
Just a little broken,
(I will mend in time)

Just a little quaint, just a little smart
A fraction of wit, a lot of heart.
A smatter of bright, too much of dull,
A glass half empty perceived half-full,

A tattle of talk who never learned how
To keep her silences, not even now.

Words are Scattered Leaves

Words are scattered leaves
With autumn colors on,
That once raked neatly in a pile
Along the wind are blown.
Tumbled in a heap
They make a crackling noise
At children buried to the eyes
In giggling little joys.
Curled in Bonnie fire
Their pungent echoes rise
On smoke that goes halooing
Across the distances.

A Budding Poet

Be careful lest you live your life in words,
Enjoy words as you would a lovely flower,
Do not build of words a lofty tower
To set you apart above the beasts and birds.

Words create enchanted worlds for you,
Grand estates where peacocks strut and spread
Exotic adjectives, hung overhead painted in words,
Are rainbows arched on blue.

But do not walk on floors of marble words,
Through empty hallways echoing their sound,
While passion chained in dungeons underground
Forgotten, screams, but never can be heard.

Children's Ward*

I remember how beautiful she was
Long brown hair spilling over her pillow,
Eyes, two big, black stars.
Her bed was so close to mine
I could hear her quiet moaning in the dark.
Sometimes a nurse would come to ease her pain.
She always spoke in a gentle voice
And always without complaint.
One night, in the yellow light from the hall,
They wheeled her by my bed.
She was dead...She was only 16...
I remember how beautiful she was.

*Highland Park, Michigan

Poems of Childhood

I just wanted to hold
The fuzzy black chick
Almost lost in the sea of gold
Chicks scurrying to and fro
In fear of me;
I reached out my hand
But he turned so suddenly
Under my foot
I could not stop
The weight of death above him.
I never told.
But afterward while playing a game,
Reading a book,
Or helping mother with some chore,
The look of that little Crushed Thing,
The eye opaque in death,
Perfect in every detail
Like a still-life photograph,
Would flash into my head.
No one understood the quick tears
In the midst of happy laughter;
Thirty years after, it comes back
At the most unexpected times.
I'm sorry.

There is a Place

There is a place with sleepy streets
Ice wagons and tire swings
Where sisters are
And brothers telling stories in the dark.
There is a place with knee-high clover,
Rusty tractor seats in barnyards,
Cousins, and wishing on a star.
A place that smells of fresh mown hay
and tea roses,
Choke cherry syrup and burnt sugar cake.
Where death is only a ghost story
Or whistling by the graveyard.
There is a place with picture windows
Rosy in the sunrise,
Steaming cups of tea,
And eyes across an old familiar room,
Where laughter is, and long remembered love.
But first–
I must cross this field of poppies.

Joey Was

I used to stand in wait
At the old school gate for Joey,
Til the bell would ring,
And children came cascading from the door,
Forevermore I will see that happy scene,
Undimmed by years that have passed between
An old woman, and a little girl of four.
He was the neighbor's boy
And, oh, the joy he put into the day;
Holding to my hand we skipped away
Laughing down the hill; I see him still.
Then, he moved away; no parting word
Just turning back he watched me out of sight,
The sound of damp clods flying
Under the old cars wheels was all I heard,
And my own crying long into the night.
Ravelled the rope that hangs from the bell
In the schoolyard, swings are empty now,
The classroom just a shell;
The gate is broken down,
Rusted and unused since they built the school in town.
Except for memory of a laughing little ghost – and me.
Forever we come as sun and wind and rain,
Forever I climb this haunted hill to pause
A moment here remembering when – Joey was.

Secret Love

"Do you suppose he cares for me?"
She heard her sisters say,
And she replied (too evenly)
"It kind of looks that way,
He brought you flowers didn't he?"
"Oh, yes, and he's so sweet,
I can't get over how he talks
And always dressed so neat;
So different from the other boys,
His gift with words and all,
Have you stood up close to him?
My gosh! He sure is tall."
"No, I never stood up close."
(These last words just a sigh)
And then from yonder doorway
A deep male voice said, "Hi!"
There he was framed by the night
Grinning like a clown,
So quick her heart jumped in her throat,
She had to choke it down.
His dark eyes were sparkling
In the lantern light.
"May I take Laury for a stroll?
It's such a lovely night."
He stood so close their fingers touched,
She quickly backed away,
In a moment she would scream,
"Yes, of course you may."
Alone she leaned against the door,
"Well, I'm glad they're gone."
And then–at last the tear drops fell.
One by One.

Random Thought

Where goes the spirit when the soul has vacated?
Does it drift like gossamer through brain cells?
Or cling, as fog clings, to masts of ghost ships a sail
on a shoreless sea...
Sounding bottom in an empty heart?

Chapter II

First Love

Love is like a mountain
Overpowering and grand,
Love is golden; sunlight on the sand,
Love, like a bird, swoops and sails
Unfettered, soaring high!
Then dips its wing–
To fall away in the sky.

Reflections

When will I grow up to match my face?
Lose this hold on youth, replace
These childish dreams with truth?
Learn that life is full of little flaws;
Thorns and roses, mud in crystal pools;
Too much faith without perspective draws
Pretty pictures in the eyes of fools.
More inclined to note the budding trees
Than dirt in gutters. Though time alter these
Reflections now with grief
It will not matter;
The mirror warped, distorts, but does not shatter.

The Stirring

You are well content with household chores,
Making beds, straightening books,
Sweeping dusty floors.
You whistle while the washer whirls,
Taking time to comb the kinks
From Janie's shiny curls,
You never once regret.
Dishes washed and put away,
Lunch time passed, cookies baked,
Just enough to fill your day,
You are satisfied – and yet,
When supper's over, lights turned low,
Out there in the night somewhere
You hear a whistle blow,
The lonely whistle of a train,
Floating through your tidy home,
You wouldn't once complain –

But your heart follows the sound until
It dances over the shadow hill,
To places exciting and new –
Calling, calling, calling –
Calling you.

Shadow Love

His eyes are blue at times
And sometimes brown,
A sea-green shade of China Jade,
Or painted, like a clown.
His, a tiger eye
In jungles of the mind,
Or eyes of purple twilight
On hidden plains of time.

Something is Haunting Me

There is something haunting me,
Something sad about the night,
The silhouette of house, old fence and tree
When the moon is bright.
To move would break the spell,
Shadowed lawn and silences
That seemed to throb and swell –
Hold back the dawn.
What hurts me so?
A mind can still retain
The beautiful when perfect moments go
And dream again.
Still, I linger here
Reluctant to depart,
Why should night and summer in the air
Break my heart?

Wartime 1943*

It was all a game–
Streetlights painted on the seaward side,
Driving with our parking lights on and dim,
Our friendly stretch of ocean was too wide
For death to cross.
Search lights swept the sky above the town
In constant vigil, and each little house
With windows draped and all the lamps turned down
A safe cocoon.

To naïve girls the danger was a lark,
Our beach, vulnerable, guarded in the dark
By armed patrols, secure in the afternoon.
The glamour of the uniform, a name
Scribbled with an APO address,
Lonely soldiers face, a sailor's kiss
Forgotten, it was all a game...

A world away in some French countryside,
A bomber hit a bridge and crashed in flame;
Death was noble, war was all a game–
Until you died.

*Venice, California

The Bridge

I walk alone to the bridge today,
The rain is soothing against my face,
I pause to watch the wild reeds sway,
And sweep the water with feminine grace.
A wistful sound, like a lonely sigh,
And mist comes into these eyes of mine,
Tracing the curve of winter sky
Over the hill where house lights shine.
It is peaceful here;
Here we met in spring, and still
It seems a cloying smell of blossoms
Hangs in the very air.
Here, as dead leaves fell we parted.
Leaves will green again though trees are bare;
Can love die, though I am brokenhearted,
If my memory greens to him–
Somewhere?

Unvital Statistics

A hundred years ago there was a spring,
Flowers bloomed, the sun touched everything.
The moon rose to bathe the earth with light,
Lovers met, parted in the night–
Just as today.
A hundred years ago somebody cried,
Laughed, kissed, made promises and lied,
Bore a grief in silence; humble clay
That lived a life unknown–
And passed away.
History ignores the mundane thing,
Records the life of genius, reign of King,
No scroll of dreams, or day that follows day,
Common little lives in disarray
Are nothing new.
A hundred years from now will be the same,
Those who love today will have no name,
The moon shall rise, springtime come and go,
A hundred years from now no one will know–
How much I loved you.

Words

What are words to me?
They cannot bring back nights of summer gold,
Nor walks through winter white;
I cannot hold
A trite, descriptive phrase,
Nor reams of verse put love into my days
Or be, what used to be.
Crumbs dropped in
Darkened wood, are words,
To mark love's maundering, a feast for crows,
A path of silly, antiquated prose
Flung innocently, flowery and absurd.
What are words to me?
I would take all the words once spoken,
Scribbled to a young heart broken,
Wrung from an anguished soul and sung
And drown them all in the sea.

Vignette

Pigeons dobbed on rooftops
Pelicans folded like muddy sails
Along the pier
Seagulls wheeling and crying
Above an empty beach
Sandpipers scurrying after crabs
In the waves ebb;
In the warmth of a California sunshine morning
My spirit soars on wings of its own.

Chapter III

Marriage

~ Part 1~

Richard "Bing" Bingo

I am the pendulum swinging
From joy to sorrow.
While the clock ticks silently
In the chamber of my days,
Through the empty hallways
Interchanging light and dark
Toll of midnight,
Chimes at morning heralding
The clear insistent singing
Of the lark.

Wedding Night

Roses made of shadows
Diamonds made of gleams
Counter pane of moon light
Faces etched of dreams
Midnight made of whispers
Rustle of assents
Consummate in satin
Love's sweet nescience

Silent Song

I knew he sang though lost the song
On this bombarded ear,
Warble moved in feathered throat,
And shimmered in the air.
He may as well be still and go
Along a calmer route,
As waste–in airport garden–notes
A silver roar drowns out.

On Progress

Take a good look at the trees
Along this old familiar street,
"Progress" say the Pharisees
(Kneeling at his cement feet)
"Needs a wider thoroughfare,"
Old friends of the neighborhood
Guillotined, and who's to care?
"It is for the greater good."
How convenient it will be,
Who will miss the leaves in spring
Of alder, elm, and who will see
Dwarf crab-apple blossoming?
We drive through the passing scene
With haste, and trees get in the way,
And houses do, and peaceful green–
We had yesterday.

A Dream of Stars*

Against the skyline bridges
String lights across the bay, and ridges
On the periphery are roped with pearls of light
From moving cars.
Signal lights are seen
Broken in the water between
Shadows of trees, the narrow river
Ripples amber, red, and green
Where once the friendly stream
Held only stars.
Rosette sequins glint and gleam
In flicker of candle on a bistro wall;
Down creaking cellar stair,
In gloomy hall,
Yellow bulbs afford a meager glare.
Gaudy streets in scarlet neon frills,
Choreographed, upon a stage of hills.
Galaxies cannot intrude
Upon this fog of light;
Solitude and lovers rendezvousing in the park,
Is only a dream of stars;
For we are children frightened by
The dark.

*Honorable mention: Joyce Kilmer Annual Poetry Contest, Pueblo, Colorado 1955

Mortal

I stand on the hilltop looking down
At lights blinking on in some little town,
The desert sand beneath my feet
Still pulses with the long day's heat.
Now a breeze is blowing
Cool on my face, and night is near,
Time is busy with coming and going,
Unaltered by my presence here.
Seeing little squares of light,
In houses, yellow windows lit
By lamps in stuffy rooms, the finite
Under heavens infinite –
It comes to me:
Little rooms – space,
Lamp light – a star,
Though we dream immortal dreams,
How mortal we really are.

Left Behind

One left–
One bird
Shivering in the field bereft,
Dragging his injured wing.
Of all the noisy, brilliant
Beautiful birds
One left–
And he has forgotten the sky,
And how to sing.

Birds Don't Stop Here
(In East L.A.)

Such a little thing, such a small desire,
To see a raven wing across the sky,
Or hear, from his perch on the telephone wire
A mockingbird sing, but he flies by.
Such a harmless wish, to see a finch's breast,
Over the feeding dish on the window sill,
The busy robin building her nest,
Swish of feather, blur of bill.
Insignificant thing, the scratching sound,
Of tiny claws that cling to the ivy vine,
And I miss sparrows skittering over the ground,
The brown hawk wheeling above this house of mine.

Nightmare

Caught in beam of headlight
On a black country road.
A dog we hit that night;
The sickening thud,
The horrible surprise of eternity frozen in his eyes.
The stain on gravel pooled and red,
Driving away grateful he was dead
Without suffering,
Not knowing what to do:
No house in sight and us just passing through.

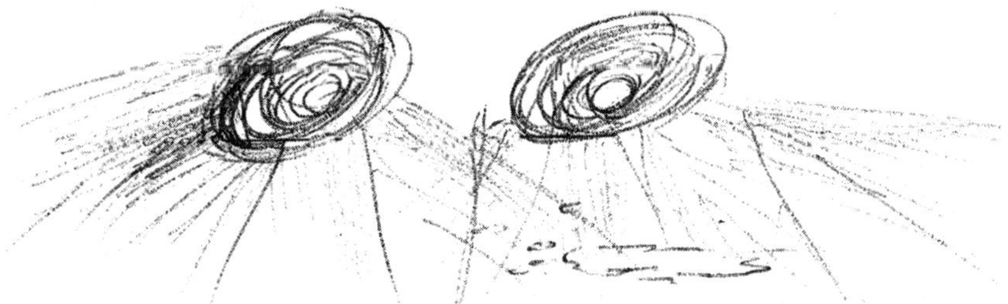

Amen

A cherry pie on the cooling rack,
And steam from the teapot curling up,
A wisp of curtain blowing back,
And sunlight on a china cup.

Lacy shade on the windowsill
Cast by the oak tree just outside,
Draped by the leaves and out again,
To spread on the meadow cool and wide.

The meadow in her summer dress,
All green and gold in the midday hour,
Orchards flung with a suddenness,
Beyond the fence moss-roses flower.

Ruts in the road still hold the trace
Of puddles after the summer rain,
A patch of sky, a dear familiar face
Reflected there, and love is home again.

Amen

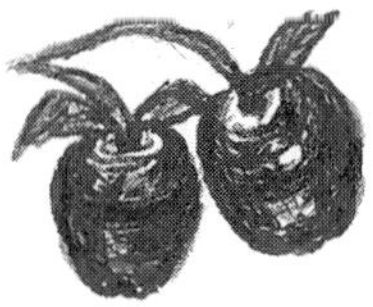

The Homestead

I will remember apples sagging down the bough,
Over the neighbor's fence instead
Of cobwebs draped in corners now
Where the mouse runs in the wall,
And casements grow dank, smelly things;
I will remember April-blown fragrances
Of our pristine springs.
Rheumy sunlight filters through
Cracked windows sickly with the stain
Of yellow dust from worn-out fields
And tardy rain.
Blackened pea-vine rattling sear in the rising wind,
Tattered ensign of a ship aground,
Above the ruins old faithful friend,
The arbor leans, rusted gate is down.
A lantern's sooted chimney, dark as doom,
Smudges of light upon a dusty table,
Done with humble industry the room,
Save one spiders weaving, gray and feeble.
I will remember coffee steaming in a cup,
Crickets singing by an open door,
Here, where paint is peeled and curling up,
I see bright sunshine on a polished floor.

The Empty Land

Wait! I know this place,
Familiar as my hand;
There was a house by the river,
Just around this bend,
In a clump of willows.
There! See nesting swallows
Where the chimneys stand?
You can see the doorstep worn by little feet,
See a mother waiting in the evening heat;
If you tarry long enough and your thoughts flow free;
Feel the sweet wild grasses waving round your knee.
Wild strawberries bloomed and spread
Beside a pasture fence,
That gated an old wagon road;
See? Where the ruts commence?
Once the ditch meandering, dry and blown to dust,
Held a trickling music;
Old times gone to rust
Like that milking pail, half buried in the sand.
Now, we but remember. See the white cloud sail?
We are drifters like the clouds–
Over the empty land.

North

Every year I'm filled with summer dreams,
When winter blanks the hill and snow is deep,
Where pale morning slants across my sleep,
I see the brook trout leap in quiet streams.

Every year when spring comes tripping back
Flinging flowers, I swear by everyone,
This time when all the noisy gutters run
With April rain, is all my soul could lack.

Green of August; field and fern,
Midas-ed in sunsets golden gleaming,
Through my senses languidly is streaming,
Shining river, after the green leaves turn.

North is Autumn aching in the eyes,
Stained-glass windows open to the mind,
Color sharp enough to strike one blind
With beauty, impaled on blue October skies.

North, a cozy fire when cold winds blow;
On ghostly nights ethereal moonlight shines,
And frozen gardens under silent pines
Sleep, in soft, still iridescence of the snow.

Lower Mesa Falls

From where we sat on the canyon wall
The river one hundred feet down
Was a deep blue-shaded green
With little silver curls breaking
Once in a while on the current,
As if an artist's swift, deft brush stroke
Of a hi-lite white rippled in the sun.
But the sound was real,
The sound of water flowing,
At once peaceful and exciting,
Images of trees breaking up on the rocks,
The roar of a waterfall echoing out of sight.
Sitting with chin on knees,
The fragrance of pine needles
And purple clover
Mixed with a lusty sweetness of damp earth,
Brought a primordial pleasure,
And love flowed between us–
Wild as the river.

The Little Cabin

The little cabin stood alone
Midst the leaners, August Moon
Ornamented straighter pine
By its chimney, changing shine
To amber on old stone.
Deeper rutted was the road
Draped along the darkened wood,
Where no footfalls, echo strode,
Faithful, next my own.
Secrets gutted out, a bliss
Vespered within emptiness,
Moonlight ribboned on the wall
Waits, the shadows call and call
Two ghosts, and seasons gone.

Mountain Summer Night

Here, in aspen grove and stands
Of lodge pole pine,
We watch stars glimmer on the lake and shine
Between the trailing fingers of our hands.
Here and there we see a golden spark
From campfires, glowing upward through the dark,
The steady drone
Of voices on the shore has died away,
And we are alone.
Only the faint flash, flash of fish
Disturbs the velvet night that wraps us round,
We drift in mirrored sky without a sound
Without a sound, and all the earthly bars
Cannot restrain enchanted lovers here,
Gliding through a universe of stars.

Timber Line

At timber line
Where the frightened conies run,
Fling my broken shadow across the sun,
Let the wind sow
These ashes over the valley below,
A sift in the purple clover
Of mortal dust,
When this agony is over.

Red Fish Lake Lilies

Drowned in this bowl of lilies
A little way out from shore,
In a tangle of green root shimmering,
Bright as an open door–
The sky, in a glimmering quickens,
Touched by a finger of breeze,
A jewel in its ringed-dark setting,
Encircled by rain-dark trees.

Earthbound

The forest is deserted,
The lake unrippled and still,
The last of the dust has settled
As campers drive over the hill.
I swim a little longer,
I float gazing up at the sky,
It seems I own this piece of earth
Encompassed in my eye.
I think, "How beautiful it is!
How free I am, how Free!"
Until I see the eagle soaring over me.

Love Letter Home

It isn't the peace of rolling hills,
Or gentle ripples in a quiet stream,
That pulls my thoughts along a homesick dream.
Its tumble and roar of water as it spills
Over to the granite mountain face and down
To canyon floor, the shout of gold and brown,
And shades of green against a teeming sky,
Where shifting, boiling, roiling cumulus fly.
Clap of thunder sounding North to West,
Lightning flash, smell of burning tree,
Raising my hair and running clean through me,
Fear, and a glorious pounding in the breast!

One Perfect Day Remembered

I will climb a mountain
Where autumn days are crisp and fair,
When at last I reach the top
I will keep climbing up the air–
That will be my dying;
Whether young and lying
On a bed of pain,
Whether old and sighing
Sitting upright in my chair.
Death will be bewildered
To find my soul is off somewhere
Wandering old skies.
For my last thought will be of you,
An autumn day, a mountain view,
The last picture in my dead eyes.

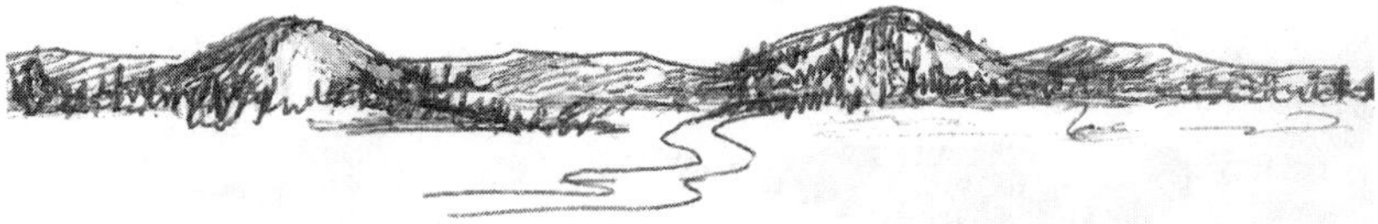

The Oak

I will be dignified in grief
Though sorrow rend the root, and strip the leaf
Flung out upon the wind–
I will not bend.
When summer is gone and all the birds have flown,
Let the willow weep in silver rain,
Trailing her limp fingers, like a stain of fragile rust,
Over the dying lawn.
Disheartened when winter gales begin,
She mourns dead roses scattered in their bed,
Delicately sad she bows her head,
Wrings her hands, and longs for what has been.
But giving shelter faithfully I bide,
Where the old house nestles to my side,
Familiar as the lonely sky, and mark
The open gate when all the panes go dark.

In its place the rose will bloom again
Beside the wall,
When robins paint the sky with tints of red
On cloudless blue
When peace as tangible as dew
Spreads over all
The earth and hints of heaven overhead.

The Dream

The trail ascending
Through the moonlit snow
And sky on the rim of the hill–
Hauntingly real.
I am returning a way I seem to know,
Feel the wind blow,
And a terrible yearning for some dear thing lost.
Patterns on blue frost
Are distant crowds
Halloing in a carnival atmosphere,
In a shadow, never moving near,
A face; forgotten in a rush of woe,
Though we parted but an hour ago...
In every eye that passed
Endlessly down the hill,
The light looked for, the one look that would tell
The momentary lost was found at last–
Is never seen.
So on and on, up some endless stair
Of moonlight, on a hill of snow
I climb; and those familiar eyes still go
Too far away for recognition here–
Moving lonely in a dream.

Languid

Blood runs sluggish in a tropic clime,
Heavy perfume of exotic flowers
Blows forever through a lump of hours,
Smothered and endless in a void of time.

Never Apart From Me*

My fingers trace your body in the dark,
You do not stir, nor is it my intent
To rouse you, all my passion spent
Is weakness in the limbs, this bed and ark
On some Sargasso Sea.
Once again we lay in love's repose,
The blood still pulsing faintly in the throat,
Damp on your brow the golden ringlets float
Over the pillow, as your eyelids close.
Never apart from me,
Though year upon year, morning on morning slip
Into the room; even beyond this world
We will endure. Now my hand is curled
Under your breast, and through half parted lips
You breathe my name.
Why do I cling to you and dread the dawn?
Treacherous eyes of mine, forebear
Weeping; love asleep beside me unaware
Comforts me... This strange foreboding gone...
Quickly as it came.

The Master Mind

Four walls your seasons had,
A ceiling and a floor,
One half-attempted window,
Never the spirit–door.
It's little narrow look
Ended at the road,
Undreamed–for lack of vision–
The mountain and the wood.

*His words in paraphrase

Were It the Same

Silent the town, the house is sleeping,
Save for me by the window weeping,
Here I will be when day comes creeping
Over the hill and down.
Off to the right in the meadow standing
Shrouded in mist or grasses bending
Toward the sun, and sunlight rending
Shadow, mist and night.
Were it the same as yesterday's dawning,
Lovely dreams mixed with the morning,
Innocent joy for the day a borning
And mother calling my name.
Were it the same, the cowbell clinking,
The woodsman paused by our well and drinking,
Bringing no pain to a young girl's thinking,
Sorrow, before you came.
I am estranged from swallows crying
Out on the wind, and the wind's soft sighing
Life goes on with blooming and dying...
I alone have changed.

RB

There would be too much of you left here,
No room without some little touch, your hand
On every cozy nook, each spacious room
The better for your loving labor; eyes
Need not look far to see the artisan,
The wine rack carved from oak, the friendly door
Painted and trimmed, apothecary shelves
Hanging in the pantry hall, and over there
The china cupboards, antique jardiniere
Among the plants you nurture carefully.
Yes, there would be too much of you left here,
I could not bear to stay and this house, too,
Would be home for strangers rather than
A tomb for artifacts of you and me.

Light akin to laser pierced my heart,
And burned across the letters of your name.
Treasures sealed away in antique jars
For centuries, down ancient wells,
In cellars rimed and dim,
Held mysteries of no more awe than this:
To cipher love with sacred hieroglyphs
A thousand times –
And understand but once.

Uncomforted

How dare you write of death
In trite, pretentious tomes;
"It is God's will," and all that old clap-trap,
The little dog that creeps into my lap
And licks my hand, expresses love more honestly
Than all of your empty poems.
Not "Gone beyond the wall" beloved smile,
Or eyes once dark with passion blank with drug
To dull the pain; saccharin words, the pious and the smug–
Are so much coprolile.
Verses penned to ease a suffering
Beyond all ease seems sanctimonious,
God thrown in my face at a time like this...
I cannot bear, just don't say anything.

Life Wasted

We have lost our importance in the scheme of things.
How much happier were we, who, at the beginning
believed our destiny intertwined with the gods.
For then to exist had meaning, to face peril was to
taste life, to conquer fear was to feel exalted, to know
with each triumph we were a little more divine.

Now, there is no action.
We are separated from the gods by sloth and comfort.
Apathy is a black hood pulled over our eyes.
No cause is great enough, no joy forceful enough to
raise us from our couches.

Our temples stand empty.

Vignette

Vagabond summer takes to roads again
Hospitable doors latch against a sudden shivering
Windows opened to June pulchritude
Now weeping occlude our friendly field.

Chapter III

Marriage

~ Part 2 ~
Seasons of Love

I learned to love and not possess,
I learned because there was no other choice,
To feel a surge of tenderness and hide it,
To see a certain face
And not visibly rejoice.
To turn from eyes gone soft with love,
And lips I dare not kiss, is only
Lessons in my abc's–
Promoted now to "lonely."

The Road

Tis only now when I am old
That I can see beyond the wood,
See the distant hills unfold,
Reflecting sky in pools that flood
The narrow ribbon of the road.
Now far behind in misty veils
Where time no longer passes through,
Forever in love's memory dwells
One fragrant April wet with dew,
Soft peal the old cathedral bells.
Tis only now when eyes grow dim
That loves sweet visions inward turn;
Where reverie brings more peace than pain,
I walk in dreams a while with him,
Trace the landscape back again
To kneel where Vesper candles burn.

Back Street

Moonlight wanes across the shade,
And on this side I wait, afraid
You will not come;
A fear that tortures all my days,
Knowing that two runaways
Must face the world they hide from.
You love me now but will you soon despise,
The sin I am, the secrets and lies?

Can an Alley Be Heaven?

How can an alley be Heaven
When it leads to an old flight of stairs,
How can gloom of a cheap, little room
Shut out world and its cares?
Darling, there isn't a palace
Furnished in silver and gold,
Could hold one tenth of the treasure
This little room can hold.
Here in the dark you embrace me,
Here, with your kiss on my eyes,
An alley is suddenly Heaven,
An hour is Paradise.

Chance Meeting

You, for whom I would have bartered soul,
So sure was I that we were meant to be,
Meeting in a restaurant years after,
Asking if I recall some unshared intimacy.
Every moment spent with you is shining
Like candles lighted in my memory,
But I know now: except for my name
And a happy hour or two –
You have forgotten me.

Fifth Season

After the heart has broken,
After the tears are shed
When all the tender words are spoken,
All the sweet love letters read–
Waiting ends, and also ended
Living for another sake;
Old wounds mend and having mended,
The heart that never again can break–
Will break.

My World

There are roads through stars.
I have traveled one.
I have been struck blind
Because I came too near the sun.
Struck blind while earth grew small,
Now all I see–
Is you, the sun, between the earth and me.
If you burn out - what then?
If shining days slip through my hands and fall–
What have I lost?
A universe is all.

If You Were Mine

If I could always kiss your troubled brow,
Be there when you'd need me,
As I need you now.
If I could reach out for you in the night,
Take you in my arms and hold you,
And in the morning light
Find you still there;
If this were mine and all else held in owe–
I would not care.

Incompatible

Don't tell me it wasn't real
Just because it didn't last;
Flowers are real, but flowers die
When summers past.
Don't say I'll get over you,
Though I study to forget;
Safe in zoos the swans remember
Sky, and feel a stirring yet
For the glide of golden marshes
Underwing; the roar of tide
Will pound in empty shell forever.
Differences, canyon wide,
Separate us, still our touching
Echoes back on every side.

Love's Promise

Your love was cathedral windows,
A promise of something tangible beyond the grave,
It was sky, and ascension of the soul.
Your love was music, color
All things beautiful in the world–
And it was brief.

Love

Love is like a mountain
Overpowering and grand,
Love is golden; sunlight on the sand,
Love, like a bird, swoops and sails
Unfettered, soaring high!
Then dips its wing–
To fall away in the sky.

Love Will Slumber

Love will slumber in the mind
As if in death it lay,
Hands folded on the breast
And centuries roll away.
Tis safer so, no pain can press
So spiteful in the tomb,
As memory awakened in,
And love still in the room.

Love at First Sight*

How vulnerable you looked
Gazing into your brandy manhattan
Eyes a brim with tears,
The din of the bar, the loud, outrageous music
Flowed, a silent river, by your ears.
I wanted to comfort you,
Sitting apart with dim, red sconce light haloing your
hair;
The crowd was forgotten, the drink in my hand
forgotten,
When suddenly you looked up,
And caught my glance across the neon glare.
We shared in that moment loneliness like pain,
Your haunted eyes, your strangely familiar smile.
Lifted me to some other plane–
As though we had loved–
And parted for awhile.

*His words in paraphrase

Encounter

I thought I saw you today,
Your hair, and the set of your jaw,
And the world started spinning away.

What would I say should we meet?
And my heart caught hard in my throat,
There on a down town street.

But he wasn't nearly as tall,
He passed and I walked on
As though nothing happened at all.

And maybe (it's so long ago)
In my need I keep looking for you,
And you're someone I don't even know.

On the Boulevard

Just a street affection
Two arms quick entwined
Kisses brushing kisses
Lighter than the wind.
Saviors on the corner
Loud the drum attend
Did I dare an army
Greeting an old friend?

Once in Awhile

Once in awhile
You cross my mind
Once in awhile
A faint impression of your smile,
Once in awhile
The touch of a hand, strong fingers
Only a touch
The glance of an eye that lingers
Not much; not much–
Once in awhile.

Yearning

You say you love me yet we never touch,
Such exquisite wanting hurts the heart too much,
Your eyes have pierced me through,
To the nether regions of my soul,
You, who held me once and made life whole,
Memory has built a shrine to you.
Idol worship is a pagan thing
Status crumble
Love set free takes wing.

Memory in Black and White

The icy air of keen November nights.
So crisp one thrust of hand or turn of head
It seems would snap a corner off the world,
Or cause the moon to shatter on the road
Stings half closed eyes and grips the lungs of two
Embracing figures, stunned against the cold.
Sword-sharp branches of the blackened tree
Have pierced the sky above some frozen stream–
Etched in stark relief on grass and stone
Ourselves, dark shadow on the glittering frost
Pinned motionless, caught forever there,
As light in diamonds, night in ebony.

The Seduction

You opened a forbidden door and it excited me.
Pleasures of the flesh I never felt before
delighted me.
I could hear the music and see the lights
of the fair,
So I followed after to taste the wonders you said
were there.
But I found a gaudy carnival pitched in the dark
and damp,
Where pipes of Pan were blowing over an
evil swamp.
The soft, sweet songs of Eros by which
I was beguiled,
Are raucous incantations now,
now eyes gone wild
Mark the bitterroot where the fox is hid,
And I hear the swift hounds baying
in the wood.

Still I Love

Summers come and go,
The dead leaves fall
On dormant grass
And rot beneath the snow.
The sapling birch grows tall
Shading the yard in spring,
And houses stand on all
The fragrant fields
Where we went wandering.
I once walked with you
Down quiet streets where shadows glide,
Here, where boulevards are wide
And traffic rushes through.
Still, the night sky teams with stars
Above the river shore,
Unchanged the lilac by the door,
Still, I love, dream my lonely dreams,
And watch for you, as I have watched before.

Promoted

I can sit and look at you like this,
Calm as a stagnant pool,
Without the giddiness of tides
Pulling at my blood,
Without the old sickness upon me.
Now we can laugh and speak of other loves,
Friendly harbors where we moored
Along our separate ways;
Without tears,
No longer clinging one to the other,
As drowning swimmers cling
To the vanishing rock.
We spend an hour anchored here
With bright sails furled
Out of the storm,
And if the current catches us again–
You or I can take the helm
Sure of the waves, guide us in–
Or steer us out to sea.

The Return*

Like storms in summer skies
Over a green and luminescent sea,
When he looked at me,
His oddly colored eyes.
Black, his hair, a rippling black
Wave of midnight on the brow,
Silvered at the temples now.
It surges back,
The tide of tenderness that drowned me then,
Flung up on some old forgotten shore,
Memories that walked this beach before,
Seeing him so suddenly again.
Now the siren song
Is heard once more in this deserted place,
Charted in his face,
Those isles of love I steered to all along.

*Published in Alura Quarterly

Eyes

Herby Dinus brown of eye,
I loved him as a silly child,
Kissed his hand and wept as miles
Blurred the wave of his goodbye.
Russell Grower's twinkled blue
With merriment, and oh, my heart
Forever ached with might-have-been!
"Lost In Action" in the war
Never to return again...
So– I married hero Jack;
Eyes of green, and sandy hair;
Such a naive, hurtful thing,
Now no longer here nor there.
But Russ came home! Too late, too late;
For I had wed and so had he,
When friends told him I didn't wait,
Thought him dead, thus dead to me...
Joe's eyes were Black, oh yes, young Joe,
Who pleased me in so many ways,
He wanted to take care of me
In common law for all my days...
Then came a sailor in a dream
I dreamed before we ever met;
Bing's eyes were brown, we shared a life
Of Three plus forty years – and yet –
Although he died, his eyes still shine
With love as last they gazed in mine.
Did he ever know of one
Whose glance from other eyes of green
Made my heart a fluttering bird,
Yearning for those heights unseen?
Once again the eyes of brown;
Emmy taught the songs to me
With humorous guile, our strange duet

A concert of cacophony...
Blue eyes again where Satan dwelled,
And sited victims one by one
Along a fence of lies, and killed
Each cooing dove with velvet gun.
Laughing blue eyes gazed once more
With love in mine, and tenderness,
Glinted moonlight on a lake,
One midnight's silken, soft caress.
The first and last, the worst and best–
I still remember now and then...
Brush of lips against my cheek,
The lover lost in mists between
Who sighed in sweet surprise to me:
"How green your eyes! How green!"

Rendezvous

Follow the road up the mountainside,
Look for the sky where the hills divide,
There is a cabin half buried in snow,
Kindle the fire, in the fire's glow
Sleep snug and warm til the storm has passed
Give in to dreams, hold them fast,
Tingle your senses with reverie,
Blow out the candle–
Wait for me.

Short Story

He kissed my lips, and he kissed my eyes
"I don't love you and never will," he said
"I belong to her and it isn't right
To sneak over here like a thief in the night,
Seducing you with a pack of lies."

He cried in my arms, and took me to bed.

"I've gone a bit crazy to be here at all,
I must take leave while the sky's still black."
He covered my breast with his naked chest,
The moon rose over the mountain's crest,
He jumped at each chime of the clock in the hall,
Fled down a secret, midnight track–

And never came back.

I Will Know*

When I am dead
And scattered on the wind,
Will you hear my voice,
Will you miss the songs
I'll never sing again;
Or will the love
We had so much of
Be forgotten.
When I am gone,
If you remember me,
Let it be like rain,
Or autumn leaves that blow
Across your window pane,
Let me drift away
Like mist on April days,
And be forgotten.
If you forget,
And time erases me,
If you find a place
In someone's heart,
Where you want to be,
If you can't let go,
Darling, I will know,
I'll set you free.

*Original Song recorded on "That's Another Story."

Passion of Love

Make a shallow rhythm
Of the wildest heart,
Lest the pound of thunder
Drive the breast apart.
Dip the oar of reason
Swiftly in the blood,
Lest the empty corpse in rue–
Call back the flood.

Chapter III

Marriage

~ Part 3 ~

Agony of Love

Another empty book
With page on page of BLANK
Ennui of imagery
Futility in INK.
The brain cannot rewind
A spool of thought unwound
Nor thread reweave
Or words ungrieve
Love's fatal wound.

Deceit

It is all deceit,
Life is just a lie,
We go down in defeat,
To die is just to die.
A diamond made of glass,
A monumental fraud,
When good things never come to pass
We blame it all on God.
How easy it must be
To claim our own dark star,
And curse a deity
For being what we are.
What is the good of you
Groveling on your knees?
Praying til your face turns blue,
Weeping til your eyelids freeze?
It ends as it begins;
No one to praise or blame,
You are the sum of all your sins,
Heaven and Hell are the same.

Destiny

Leaves in the teacup,
Lines in the hand.
Stars in a horoscope,
Writing in the sand.
Fortune in the deck of cards,
Gypsies telling all.
Love forever gazing,
In her crystal ball.
Chanting of the ancients,
Tribal holy man.
Scattering the dusty bones,
Reading in a scan.
Who will ride the pale horse?
Parables and scriptures,
Planets in their course.
Diagrams and ciphers,
Chart, and rising sign.
Who is master planner
Of the grand design?

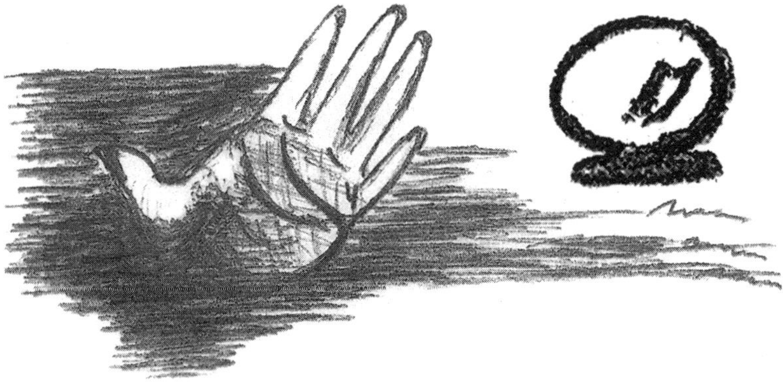

Love Aftermath

I have closed my life to you, don't call.
The days we knew are shut away.
Let years befall,
I will not look at them again,
Nor stir up tender, little scenes
To cause me pain.
Oh, love, just one last look,
One look at love the way it used to be,
Before the sleepless nights,
The tear stained book,
Before your leaving changed it all for me.

Life never really changes at all;
It's spring again.
Again the blustery winds
Sweep skies of snow before the April rain.
I would not have believed a year ago
I could withstand the anguish and survive,
But here I am without you, still alive–
I don't know why, it's spring,
That's all I know.

Droseraceae

You are cruel–
Cruel in the utmost way,
With sticky words you set the trap,
Smiling, you devour your prey.
I could not see–
Stepping from a darkened room
Into dazzling light,
The lovely garden touched with blight,
The tendrils meant for me.
Naïve heart–
Heart caught unaware,
Feels love throbbing out in sudden fright,
Sees your petals closing on the air.
Foolish to the end–
Brain squeezed dry and torn asunder,
Thinking as my eyes go under:
"Sundew will not feed upon a friend."

Take Me

Love, take me by the hair!
Wrested, vanity surrenders,
Drag me anywhere.
Don't drift over me like dew
Then vanish,
Let me know that I belong to you.
Dispense with all verbal thrust and play,
Inability to feel joy
Or even pain, holds dominion now,
Resurrect my senses and I vow
To die gladly if you ask me to.
Flesh, know thine enemies;
Intellect for one; reason,
Passion on her knees,
Fear, and ever heir thereto.
Love, for flesh, for madness and my sake,
Draw your sword and run this
Coward Through!

Unspoken

"This is the longest walk I will ever take"
He said, as he walked away from me.
How cold I must have seemed to let him go
Without a sign, but I was not free
To call him back, and so–
I stood there stricken;
As a queen held prisoner in the gaol
Cannot denounce her throne to save herself,
And waits in silence for the axe to fall.

The Passing Days

We hunted rabbits in the sage,
Was it last winter or the winter before?
Up to our knees in snow and laughing,
Alive in every pore.
I almost forgot what the world was like
That dazzling morning in the sun,
Memories I wanted to keep forever,
I have wept out of me one by one.
Now I sit in the house through winter
Watching the passing days,
And of them, all I can remember
Are the different shades of grays.
How odd that with your going away
All the beauty of life should flee,
The world outside is the same, I guess,
But never the same to me.

Warfare

I am under siege...
All the dreams I cannot bear to dream
Are at the gate, one long and silent scream
Rings in my head; an arsenal of years
Won't keep you out, nor will a moat of tears.
I dare not sleep...
The enemy is beating down the door,
Dead in pools of shadow on the floor–
My loyal strengths, that in the day hold fast
I alone must face the blow at last.
A kingdom lost...
Your army scales the bulwark of my brain,
Morning light creeps up the window pane,
Again embattled heart lies dead as darkness dies;
Slain by memory of your cruel, cold eyes.

Lost Heart

Some people walk around without a heart
They left it somewhere:
On a stretch of moonlight beach
More than twenty years ago,
Up the lonely mountain side
In a late December snow:
On a park bench in the square
Underneath bright sunny skies,
In an empty high school hallway
Drowning in two brimming eyes...
Everyday thoughts travel one more mile,
Bodies function in the same old way,
Suddenly, in the middle of routine,
The lost heart beats a bittersweet remembering–
From yesterday.

Equinox

Look at me in softer light,
Let me be your age tonight,
Though the Indian summer wanes
In October's scarlet lanes,
Time stands still for me when I am with you,
And autumn leaves can paint your sky
A deeper blue.

Look at me in softer light,
Let love be a bridge tonight,
From the maple turning red,
To the lamplight on your bed,
Where our shadows meld upon the wall,
And touch with fire this dying leaf–
Before I fall.

Desert

An ocean once stood here,
Love in torrents tear by tear,
Storming inward year by year.

Water fathoms deep,
Moon tides moving into sleep,
Crashing on the rampart steep.

Passions ebb and flow
Stronger than the undertow,
In the heart lashed to and fro.

Now recedes the flood,
Beached, the cargo in the blood,
Long becalmed the Tempest mood.

Deserts ask for this:
Just the drowning in a kiss,
One drop of remembered bliss.

A pool can hold the sky
Wherein lonely stars may lie,
A splash of light to catch love by.

Old Flame

I transcend this place,
I feel no disgrace
Stale beer, drunken cheer
I go on singing.
Tomorrow I will play
Somewhere down the way,
Sleazy room, greasy spoon café.
It doesn't really matter,
One stage is like another,
And there by chance,
I may run into you;
Through the smoke and din,
Some night you might walk in;
That hope keeps me going
All the long hours through.
Like a breath of spring,
In all the songs I sing,
Seamy years, bitter tears,
Echoed footsteps
In a darkened hall.
I keep you in my heart
That is why I stand apart
And rise above it all.

Portrait

We might have been a painting on the wall
For all the movement that we made;
Inanimate objects hung in a downstairs hall:
Two chairs, a table, lamp with a paper shade,
And you and I staring at our hands.
Two lumps of gray dobbed there, and slightly flat
Notes of the silly violins
Marking loves demise coldly as that.
Wells of your eyes abrim with me before,
Empty, save all you had left unsaid,
While I gaze stupidly at the gloves I wore,
And wished I were dead.
Odd, how this one memory keeps clinging;
Verdant ivy to the crumbled stone,
Trembling lip, rush of hot tears stinging;
I feel it now though years have come and gone.
How carelessly I love, and toss away
Traceries discarded in the mind;
One masterpiece of one dark yesterday
Hangs here: Portrait of Regret
Unsigned.

What Would I Do?

What would I do in case of fire,
If lightning struck, or the roof caved in?
If the dam burst, say, or you were a liar?
Tuck my knees up under my chin,
Hope the flames wouldn't burn any higher?
Pull the covers over my head,
Pretend you meant all those words you said?
What would I do if water rose
To the second floor and the chairs swirled by?
Would I wring my hands, whine and cry,
Hide in the closet? Or just suppose
The temperature dropped and everything froze,
Would I care if my heart had turned to ice?
Would I scream at loves ghost and beat the bed,
Hate you, hate you and wish you were dead,
Pretend I just misjudged you somehow?
Or weep in my hands, as I'm doing now?

Treason

The blue heron flies
Across our eyes
While we lean on the hoe
Unaware of the crow
That pecks out the seed behind us.
His brothers arrive, now two, now five
By the hundreds they drop,
Devour the crop,
Black out the sun and blind us.
The scarecrow stands
Flapping his hands,
With a head full of straw
And denies what he saw,
As feathers of death above him
Fall to the ground.
Only the sound
Of blue heron wings
In the distance sings
To the peasant who foolishly loved him.

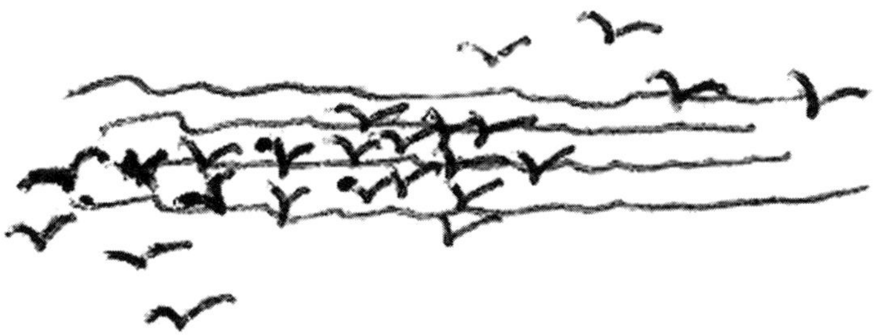

Those Were the Years

1969

That was the year men walked on the moon,
"Games People Play" was a popular tune,
The farmers burned crops to force up the prices,
X-rated films were the "Thing" to entice us.
(And that was the year we laughed in the sun,
In a town in Montana; the year my heart knew
Exquisitely sweet December days,
The still, white world of two runaways)
That was a year I loved you.

1970

"Snowbird" was one of the hits of that year,
Jet planes were sky-jacked and burned in Algiers,
The pope could be seen every where but in Rome,
Our crippled spaceship came limping back home.
(And, Oh, September! I'm living it yet.
To wake in your arms, what more could there be?
The stir of desire, the sweet caress,
The heights of all loving, the depth of your
tenderness)
That was a year you loved me.

1971

That was the year of the long goodbye,
The year of the writing on the wall.
The year we knew we must end it all.
The one last kiss, the sad regret,
The tears, and the swearing we'd never forget–
That was the year...

Soon

I will be free of you, my dear,
Soon, and it will be good to know
I can walk the beach at dawn,
Watch the night tide ebb and flow,
And not care that you are gone.
I will forget you were once here
In the fall of virgin snow,
Laughing with your great-coat on,
Or sailing blue summers long-ago.
I will forget that all I own
Of love's estate lies harbored here.
I will be free of you, my dear,
Your boat moored on the rocks below,
Your memory locked in the cottage here
By an empty sea–
(If not this year, in a year or so).

Let Nothing Matter

"Let nothing matter more than it should,"
You said to me, and so I tried
Not to care when our old dog died,
"An old dog does not matter," I lied.

"There's nothing to be done," you said,
"The job fell through and what's the sense
To get yourself all nervous and tense?"
"You're right," I said, "What's the difference?"

"You're acting like a child," you sneered,
"Because your songs were turned down flat,
Forget it, you tried, and that is that."
"Yes, I was thinking through my hat."

"Try to be practical for once!"
You snapped, "We can't afford the shop,
In these hard times it's bound to flop."
"Sorry, this foolishness will stop."

"What has happened, have you no pride?
Going til noon in a state of undress,
No makeup, and your hair is a mess."
"Pardon me for my carelessness."

"Why are you leaving, are you insane?
Tell me life has not been good,
I'd miss you, Dear, you know I would."
"Let nothing," I said, "matter more than it should."

Living the Lie

Under the glaring ceiling light you lean
Over an empty plate and drain your cup,
No table, but the world, lies in between
Your chair and mine. You finish standing up,
You stall for time on some pretended chore,
While I retire to our small loft alone,
You slip on your coat and mumble out the door.

Returned to darkness and a cold hearthstone,
I hear the creaking of the bottom stair,
Steady my breathing as if fast asleep.
I know where you have been, but do not care.
Tears I hide, you won't see me weep.
Vanished the Camelot we held so dear,
A hovel stands among the ruins here.

Hate

I hate with the searing hate
That burns a hole in my brain,
Clenches my teeth til the pain
Is sharp in the ears.
It took some forty years
To fill me to the brim,
Now I taste such bitter hate when I think of him
I wish I could die and be at peace again.
Oh, what a sorry sight I am when mornings come,
Hate throbbing on like a drum
Sets in my face;
Just one tiny trace
Of softness in the eyes;
But the mouth is tight, the heart is hard, for all those lies,
Would then I were stricken blind and dumb.
I do not wish to see this lump of flesh,
The curving lines puffed out and gone to seed,
Sitting in the house like some brown weed
Thrust through the floor,
Nor thinks, nor feels the way it did before,
Nor tears to quench this hate,
No wounds to bleed.

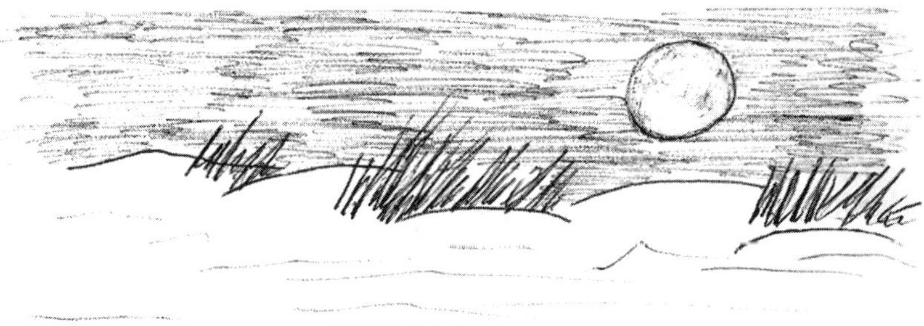

A Rhyme*

Shadowed dune was like old pewter,
Summer moon on white sea sand,
Broken tune from the pavilion,
Lost in surf along the strand.
Lanterns hung above the board walk,
Sequins strung on velvet sky,
Out among the tall sea grasses
Whispering, walked you and I.
Silken shawl dropped and forgotten,
Lonely call of wheeling bird,
Rise and fall of wild wave crashing
In our breasts was all we heard...
Mountain lake and sunset burning
In the break of wave onshore,
Sudden ache of love remembered;
Sound of sea forever more.

* Published in Alura Quarterly

This Is All

This is all that's left of him,
Shadow in a veil
Of midnight fog and moonlight,
Two hands gripped on the rail.
This is all that's left of him,
A glance at open sea,
A wounded flutter in the eyes
Is all that's left of me.

Chapter III

Marriage

~ Part 4 ~

Family and Friends

Goodness has nothing to do with duty;
Guilt does, and has to do with everything,
It has to do with getting old doing your duty
Knowing you will never be free.

Mother

I did not think of you as lilacs, lavender and lace
Rather, the rock on which our mansions stand,
A sheltered cove along the stormy strand,
Sustenance and home, a safer place.
Your eyes were never limpid pools of light,
Mirrors to reflect the face of God's,
But piercing truth; if courage could be seen.
Your eyes held all the courage of a queen
Who keeps her realm intact against all odds.
Times were hard, life never free of care,
Sometimes there was not enough to eat,
Sometimes you waged war against despair.
Now the leaves desert the gnarled tree,
Your daily strengths deserting one by one,
Yet Autumn, dying, leaves a meager sun;
One yesterday, burned in my memory:
You at the cabin standing, in light from the open door,
Searching the dark road up and down,
For two lost girls, and from the town–
The surge of joy when we saw you there
Will be with me forever more.
If the pathway of life be narrow or wide
Whether friends be false or true,
If we cross the bar in robes of white,
Or as shades long grieving in shrouds of night
Silently filing through,
You will be there, at the end of that long dark road
With the light shining behind you.

Father

You always seemed much taller than you are
Larger-than-life to me,
As though you had visited some distant star
Or fathom the depth of the sea.
Are you laughing at that, old partner?
You never pretend to be more than you seem,
Give you a line to cast in the stream,
Your dream of the Mother Lode
And you're content, the realm of all outdoors is your abode.
You can laugh at an earthy joke,
Tell stories along with the best;
Your spirit reminds me of summer smoke,
That hazes the hill, purples the slope, colors the sky down to the west.
Oh, you can be downright ornery,
Old-fashioned-set-in-your-ways,
But you leap the craggy steep of yesterdays
To blaze the trail into eternity.
As long as the salmon are running,
Long as the mountains stand,
You will face the bend in the river,
You will turn a rock in your hand.
The trails will miss you as much as we,
The hills that call you by name,
Somewhere beside a quiet stream,
When you slip down to that last, long dream.
The Maker will stake you a claim...
As long as hearts feel love and remember,
As long as the seasons roll,
If beauty endure through the ages,
Your soul will endure in my soul–
My father.

Heart of the Pioneer

They left the valley settled in green,
To cross horizons for places unknown,
To rebuild dreams all scattered and flown,
To conquer the West, conquer their fear,
That was the heart of the Pioneer.

The wheels turned 'round, the wagons creaked,
Jogging along over rivers and rocks,
Comfort shut up in a wooden box,
Their bodies exhausted, their memory too clear,
Weary the heart of the Pioneer.

Over the hill past the prairie grass,
They crawled across desert left over from hell,
Blazing sun made their dry tongues swell,
They prayed, "Let there be water near"
To freshen the heart of the Pioneer.

Came night when stars were close as a kiss,
And man had a promise of love to keep,
When mothers crooned their babes to sleep,
The firelight glow made these moments dear,
Instilled in the heart of the Pioneer.

Morning brought heat, and the savage yell,
Lips that kissed neath a midnight moon,
Were bloody and still in the dust of noon.
Good men died on their women's breast,
Torn from those arms they were laid to rest,
Under the sand all freckled with tears,
But brave were the hearts of the Pioneers.

The mountains came, the pines were tall,
Lakes were deep, and rivers wide,
They cut their way up the mountainside,
Singing God's praise with joy sincere,
And full was the heart of the Pioneer.

Colors were splashed on the autumn morn,
They sweat and swore and worked all day,
Howls of the wolf pack circling prey,
Brought alarm on the keen night air,
Tormenting the heart of the Pioneer.

Time was short, the winter came,
Bringing snow and the icy breath,
Wagons were covered with crystal death,
Wildlife fled, brave men cried,
While their women starved, and their babies died,
They cursed, and prayed, for skies were drear
Chilling the heart of the Pioneer.

Gone is the creak of the wagon wheel
Gone is the cry of "Wagons Roll!"
Scattered, crumbled, and whirled away
Like pages from diaries of long ago,
But never the dream, never the goal...
Now, when life humbles me, this is my prayer
Give me the heart of the Pioneer.

Farm Scene

I gather it all in; apples in the bin,
Pitchfork tossing hay
For gray mare and the Bay.
In the stanchion stands
Milk cow, as strong hands
Pull a foamy stream
We separate the cream
In vats kept frosty cold.
Snake lies in a fold
Beside the milk house door,
Cat slinks cross the floor,
Extends her hidden claws
In that moments pause
Rafter owl swoops down,
Snake and owl are one
In flap of feathered wing
And reptile's slithering.
Mare turns whitened eyes
Toward the sound and shies
Her rump a distance right,
Cat leaps out of sight.
All around the farm,
Chickens squawk alarm.
Behind the rippling grain
I see the distant rain
Sheeting to the ground
Windmill whirring round,
Hear the splatting sound
Of rain on roof
And watch the storm gray out the pond.

Embroidered Spring

Slowly the yellow grass turned green,
Embroidery of a spring time scene,
Leaves bunched on a brown cotton tree,
Stitched with thread from memory.
Sweet peas on a variegated vine
Changed the color line by line,
A cross-stitched trellis marks the hem
By the print of an unfinished holly hock stem;
Lilacs leaned their purple and white
Along the edge and out of sight.
The French-knot face of a daffodil
Bloomed in her lap, and the needle was still,
Trembling fingers released the ring
That held a part of her hand-made spring.
She smoothed the cloth with a tired sigh,
Glimpsed a daydream slipping by,
Could almost hear the children call
From the yard as they did when they were small,
As she leaned on the open window sill
To watch the traffic thread the hill...
From the old folks home where her days were spent,
She heard the city's sad lament,
Saw the factories grim and gray,
And wondered, "Where do the children play?"
She yearned for a lung full of country air
Where the meadows reached to anywhere;
But wishing made her old eyes sting,
So she tried not to think of anything.

Nine Years Going on Ten

Nine years going on ten
The doors swing out, the doors swing in,
The daughters come but she can't recall
Who pushed her wheelchair down the hall;
Her son brings her flowers but the flowers die
For lack of water, and weeks go by,
And the doors swing out, the doors swing in,
Nine years going on ten.
The doctor comes to check her sight,
And her bladder tube isn't draining right,
They bring her pills in a paper cup;
A grandchild visits to cheer her up
With pictures of the family,
The newest branch on the family tree,
And a kiss for the cheek of an old grandmother,
Who can distinguish one face from another.
She bruises herself, and she suffers a stroke,
The nurse can't remember when last she spoke,
But her speech comes back, and it starts again,
Nine years going on ten.
She asks for her brother but her brother is dead,
And she can't remember the tears she shed
On hearing the news three years ago.
She wants to go home but they tell her no,
We live too far, or it's starting to snow,
And maybe they'll take her another day,
So she forgets and they go away,
Thinking they can't bear to visit again,
Nine years going on ten.
Nine years going on ten,
The doors swing out, the doors swing in,
She thinks her mother dropped by for tea,
(But her mother's been gone since '83)
And they set on the porch and had a nice chat,

Now she is calling her long dead cat.
She takes to her bed and she's trembling and white,
Her children don't think she will live through the
night,
But the nurses are there with the shot and the pills,
In the medical know-how in case her heart fails,
They watch her suffer, they wonder why,
And their eyes turn up to a silent sky,
While the old folks go out,
And the new folks come in–
Nine years going on ten.

Prognosis

We share a quiet moment in the hall,
Your smile is down, you drop the brave facade,
For we can read the writing on the wall,
And holding trembling hand we speak of God.
Closer now, no curtains of pretense
Drawn over guarded eyes, no measured speech
To spare the other pain, just love intense
And true enough to span the bitter breach
Between your old worn-out heart and mine.
I see the unshed tears, how bright they shine,
In eyes once granite hard, with flint like strength,
The fight gone out one minutes' half a length–
And turn away; painfully aware:
More lame am I than you trapped in your chair.

The Umbilical Cord

It stretches clear across town
From south Grand Avenue to Maple Street;
It lies along the parkway
Where dogs sniffed at it,
Worry it with cautious paws.
It is draped on the road like a traffic counter,
And cars run over it.
It gleams in the summer grass;
Sheathed in ice hidden under the snow,
It is frozen to the pavement in winter,
And nobody knows.
It is the cord on the telephone.
The fifth commandment cylindrical.

Legacy

How does one stop the dreadful thought
Of cruelty to a poor, defenseless child?
Trust, and need for a mother's love defiled
By her ignorance, and what that ignorance wrought?
Can one forgive the angry blow, the shout,
The eyes that looked but never really saw
Such loneliness, or notice light withdraw
From innocent eyes, sputter and go out?
Can I forgive you, mother,
For old wounds inflicted carelessly?
Can my boy where ever he is now,
Find forgiveness in his heart for me?

Frank
(My son)

Angry young man pacing
Football letters droop dejectedly from shoulders.

Not chosen today for glory
His pride is a pennant in the dust.

Elders unperceiving think
It's only a game.

~~~

Some other time
When I have time to spare
I will paint you just the way you look
With sunshine on your hair.
Prussian blue with little flecks of white
Would match your young eyes,
Purple shadow for the depth,
And in the depths a spark of light.
To transfer love from heart to hand, to brush,
Cannot be done in haste if done at all,
Capture the wood thrush without the song?
Better to have let the palette fall:
Oh, little bird, you could not wait for time,
While I rush to gather canvas,
Oils, prepare the brush,
You are lost in the sun
And I hear the song in some tomorrow–
Where you climb.

~~~

Jack
(Five Year-Old Son)

Tucked beneath the coverlet he lies
Slumber coaxing shadow down his eyes,
Pulling silken lashes to their bed
Against his wind-blown cheeks flushed apple red.
Treasured toys that live for him in play,
Sit lifeless now until another day,
When tasseled shirt, Sheriff badge and vest,
Adorned the puffed expansion off his chest,
And other midget Cowboys turned to run
Away from smoking justice of his gun;
Or yelping Indians don their savage mail
Just visible above the back porch rail.
Now he's snug and warm beneath the spread,
One little fist is curled beside his head,
Forgetting in the night to be a man.
The little boy comes back in sleep again.
When he has grown, and childhood put away,
My heart will keep him as he is today.

Jill
(My daughter)

You are beautiful
Like a flower, or a bird,
You are all the poems ever written,
You are all the songs ever heard.
The brilliant butterfly
Emerging from the drab cocoon
That once was I.
A part of me–
From the homely bramble blooms
The rose,
From storms and drowning rains
The bright rainbows...
You are all—all I wanted to be.

Mekell
(My granddaughter)

A ray of sunshine crawled cross my floor,
A little song that warms a grandma's heart,
You were my baby for a little while,
No matter the days or years that we're apart.
Your first words here, your first steps taken too,
Now empty my arms, empty this old house,
My tears are falling on a little shoe,
For you have forgotten me, sweet "Mekell-Mouse."

Jack
(My grandson)

Brief encounters don't tell anything
You know I am your grandma and we cling
Self-consciously in a quick hello;
Just when I think we might be friends you go
Back to your home across so many miles,
Soon a boy grown one year older smiles
From his next semester photograph.
After you're gone, some pieces out of your laugh
Twinkle and break in corners of the yard
Where we hid Easter eggs; a little shard
Of last year's visit handed back to me,
Bright as your tangled kite in the apple tree.

Chandra
(My granddaughter)

Dear Granddaughter;
Today you are one year-old.
I wasn't there
To see your birthday cake
And presents everywhere,
I wasn't there in the room
But I could see
Those round button eyes
Shining up at me.
Were that all I could have
I would take it gratefully–
Happy Birthday.

Lynda
(My niece)

Your shining face is what we will remember,
Blithe spirit, haloed by your hair
Once boldly shining, faith and trust ashining
In your eyes, tho shadowed now with care.
Without fear, you trudge the pathway chosen,
Never veering from the inner light,
Down the years your little griefs were frozen
Unborn thoughts, for "God will make it right."
You believe, and fill us with a pity,
To see angelic youth and beauty dim,
In exchange for promises of heaven,
The golden voice sings homages to Him.
Suffering pangs of sadness mixed with envy,
Doubters fallen from your radiant sphere,
Longing for more earthly things familiar–
We turn from you, and seek ourselves elsewhere.

Why Do I Seek You Now?

(Emery Widowson)

Is it the lack of you this side the Veil,
The absence of a time forever flown?
Our silhouette against the moon half gone,
Cut out, and only hollow space to tell.
You once stood here?
Is it your memory hurrying to let go,
The tune played out we thought would never end?
I hear the brush of dark wing fluttering;
Old friend,
Tell me somehow, what I have need to know.

Mom Bingo
18 -- – to 1945

I see the porch of the old farmhouse,
It's once brave paint yellow and peeled away
By the harsh, eternal sun.
And just beyond, a sky so alive with cumulus clouds,
That any moment they will sail
Over the edge of the cracked and faded photograph.
A toddler in the foreground rides in a crude cart
Pulled by some long forgotten family pet,
And urging dog along,
Blurred features of his face vaguely familiar,
A gangling brother of 12 peers into the afternoon...
What stings the eyes of that tot now grown,
Like the bite of the Kansas wind–
Is your shadow before the camera,
Falling toward them over the prairie grass.

Soul Tormented
(MT)

The corridor is long and dimly lit,
There upon the threshold
You gave no lingering thought to it.
Now your step is weary,
Shadows crush and smother,
Endless seems the journeying
From one door to another.
Doors that open to a warmer place,
Where sunlight for a little while
Shines upon your face...
You do not tarry there,
Nor can love within this room
Hold you to the cheery hearth for long.
Why does sunlight in your world seem wrong,
Love that turns intense so hard to bear?
Life becomes a prison to your dreams,
You curse the fetid air and beat at bars.
Hanged from rocky parapets of time,
You dance upon the wind, and clutch at stars.

I Had a Friend
(RW)

He played piano down at the local pizza parlor,
Everyone knew his name.
He died last week.
Some of us looked sad,
Or clucked our tongue and said,
"Too bad."
But when the services were held
Nobody came.
I wanted to,
I meant to send flowers,
But they buried him in a matter of hours,
And I had other things to do.
I never thanked him for being a friend,
And "thank you" is so easy to say;
But – why talk about it now?
He can't hear <u>me</u> anyway.

Don't Count Me

I do not count myself among the lonely
Accompanied as I am by beauty; autumn in the rain,
Doe eyes peering from the quiet wood;
Poet voices; Omar, Keats, Lord Tennyson,
William Shakespeare in a sonnet mood.
(The buck approaching through the trembling trees)
Millay, Christina, Teasdale, Dickinson;
(Thoughts that make me go weak in the knees).
In a lighter vein, I reach for Parker,
Ogden Nash and all the lesser bards,
I do not count myself among the lonely.
(Til flesh, remembering, aches for more than words).

Chapter III

Marriage

~ Part 5 ~

Life on the Road

Flat on desert floors, in and out of doors,
Wide in cities, thin between
Mountains everlasting green–
The road runs.
To and back again, dusty country lane,
Soft and sandy by the sea
Footpath muddy in the rain.
Highways twist away, east by night, west by day,
Here to there, and I go where
The road runs.

Trip to Nashville

I am there in the mirror on the wall,
I am there in the vanity glass,
And there, in a briefcase by the bed,
Is the sum of all I am, or was.
This hotel room is an alien ship
Set down on a foreign star,
To breathe comes hard when I venture out,
And the hype of it all is a lonely bore,
I will sit in some office again today,
While a cool receptionist young and fair,
Sees a woman who's past her prime,
Wonders, "What is she doing here?"
The hair has silver glints in the red,
And I smile to lift the years between,
It comes like a blow to the back of the head:
Who cares what I have done, or been?
I stand with my hopes in a scrap of song,
A little success left over from youth,
A yellowed column, a tape or two,
Struck blind by the unkind light of truth.
I start to sweat, wanting to run,
And asked myself why I give a damn,
For the folks back home? To say I tried?
Or find out myself who I really am.

Miles City, Montana

The road leading down to the river
Is the same as it was back then,
The bridge is the same, and muddy water,
In spring run-off again.
This time the lilacs are curled and brown,
Fluff from cottonwoods drift in air,
Spring is a little bit older this year,
Along the crowded streets of town.
But all the excitement of "Bucking Horse Day"
Is here, on another bright morning in May.
In the shade of the tall stone pillar
That marks the fairgrounds gate,
I see the crowded grandstand,
The blue Montana sky.
All about me is silence, except for a car going by,
Then a roar of the crowd goes up,
And I can envision it all again;
Two people perched on the rail, and laughing,
(Two straws blown away on the wind).
All my remembering won't change today;
The chutes, the track, the whitewashed fence
Look the same, but, oh, how deeply I feel it,
That one small difference.

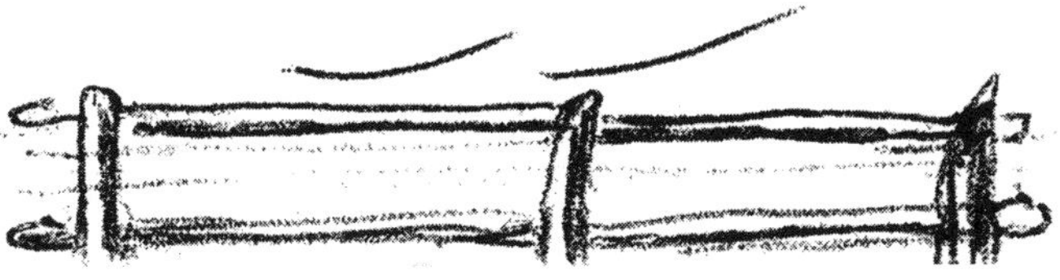

Newport, Oregon

The bonfire shared with laughing friends
Less than half an hour ago,
Falls in upon itself below
The Rocky Palisade.
We linger on the empty beach
As dawn breaks grey above the sand,
One last good night is roundelayed
Homeward down the strand.
Tell me, do you still think of it,
Those summer nights of revelry?
Eating chowder at "Mos" on the wharf,
Naming stars by the sea?
The smell of fish and wet salt air,
The little bar where we gathered round
A powdered lady with carrot-dyed hair,
Dressed in a prewar gown?
She sat at an old piano
And old songs were all she could play,
It hurt to look at the ancient face
Whenever she smiled our way.
I wonder, would she be playing still
Should we return tonight?
And waves that lap at the waterfront
Dance with the same old light?

Life most times is merely happenstance,
We meet and part,
Vow we won't forget and cross our heart,
Yet if we meet again tis just by chance.
But I shall thank them and blow a kiss
If ever I'm passing through,
For I remember them everyone,
(And I remember you).

Mine

Mine, the alabaster night
Shine of snow in the cold starlight,
Line of fence posts by the road,
Pines shivering in the silver wood,
Deep silence over the earth,
Heap of embers on the hearth,
Leap of firelight on the pane,
Sleep, and love when I wake again.

Petersburg

How far away is Petersburg?
Two thousand miles by plane?
I really don't know, but I wish we could go
Over those islands again.
Down through Wrangle Narrows,
Skimming the frigid sea,
For waiting there in a patch of sunlight
To welcome you and me–
The one little place in all this world,
Where we laughed for awhile and were free.
Crystal clear and clean, the chill Alaskan air
Surrounding this lovely jewel, and emerald green–
The water There.
Quaint little shuttered houses stand
On pilings along the slough,
Where tides rush through,
The ebb and rise
Familiar to me as the look in your eyes,
Lines in the palm of my hand.
I see it all again:
Umbrellas bob along old winding streets,
Pouring down on metal roofs in sheets,
The cold spring rain.
Seine boats freshly painted
Freed of winter rust
Crab pots–
Mended and piled high in vacant lots,
Sunshine changing mud in roads to dust.
We used to drink 'Blue Northers'
Out at Beachcomber Inn
On foggy nights,
Watch the ferry boats glide by
Their glimmering lights

Ghostly in the mist,
And watch the day begin.
We strolled every lane in the village
Each curve of rocky shore,
We learned to know each other better
Than anyone knew us before.
My feelings soar within me now
Whenever I think of you,
As Eagles used to soar in heavens blue,
The way your hair looked, and your laugh
Behind that smile I captured once
In a photograph...
I miss you, my dear companion,
Today we are worlds apart;
How far away is Petersburg?
It is here in my heart.

Boulder Dam

To the Gulf of California
Cross the burning desert floor,
The ancient Colorado.
Dumped its water on the shore
In a narrow gorge we chained her,
And I'll never be the same,
It ain't just mud that stained her,
With the color of her name.
In the blinding sun I'm clinging
To the rocky canyon wall,
I keep blastin', I keep drillin',
I keep praying' I won't fall,
Don't look down, you Cherry Picker, there
Two thousand feet below
Roaring, rushing waters
Of the Colorado flow.
Seems I grow to this jack-hammer,
And I'm burned and battered numb,
But a dry land cries for water
And we gotta give'er some.
I've been drunk, I fought and gambled,
From Scagway to Yucatan,
Been labeled "Lady Killer"
And I called myself a man
But it's here a man is rated,
Here where dyin' is a cinch,
If a drop's miscalculated
Inch by inch by inch.
I panned gold up in high country,
Brought me in a dry cat well,
Mined the coal in Pennsylvania
In the corridors of hell,
But to build a cement mountain,
Out of steel and mortal clay,

Change a river's course forever,
Though it kills a man a day,
That's what I call doin' something
The rest seems mighty tame;
When they call you "Cherry Picker"
You're a man, you earned the name.

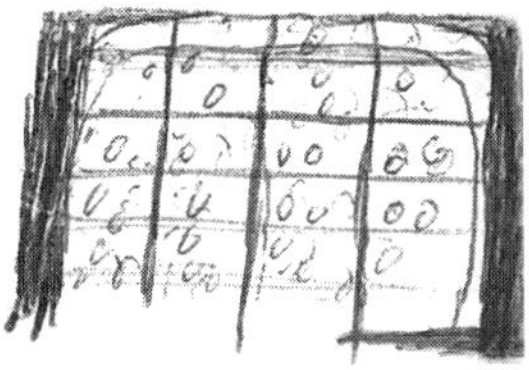

The Inn

Wine sparkling in two glasses
Logs burning in a massive stone fireplace
Snowflakes falling feather-thick past
Windows cathedral–ceiling high.
Staircase parting wavelike up the lobby wall,
Sunshine buttering toasty quilts
Mornings after the storm.
Raven in a dead tree.
Snow Angels of Ravens in the blinding
White of the road.
Claws of Ravens clacking on tin roofs
Dogs, big and friendly, sniffing at
Pant legs, or sleeping in the sun.
Snowmobiles darting in and out of
Streets white tunneled,
Headlights klieging on
Doors of cozy, crowded bars
In winter's early dark...
Why now, far away in a half sleep remembering–
Do I see only the ravens?

Three Chord Guitar

Lord, why did you give me
A heart full of memories
A head full of tunes I can't put on paper
Cause I can't recamember
One note from another
I just hear the sounds and know where they are.
I hum something clever or feel kind of hurting,
And pick out a tune on a three chord guitar...
If I'm down to a quarter, and fresh outa whiskey,
For a pound or a penny, or hot cupa coffee,
I will sit me right down and sing you a few,
Even a rock star obliged with a concert,
And kept me in clover a minute or two...
I don't think too much on the why or the wherefore,
Just open my mouth and the words tumble out,
It's fun to be sittin' around in a circle
With clever musicians, who call themselves "Pickers,"
'Cause they seem to know what the music's about.
Sometimes they asked me to give them a winner,
They're gonna be cuttin' a session come spring;
So I throw out some lines
'Bout a green country singer,
Who winds up on skid row,
'Cause he lost his first sweetheart
To a handsome young swinger,
Then I cut it myself and it makes me a star.
It's fun for a while
Then a year or so later,
I'm playin' some gig in a neighborhood bar;
Hopin' my royalty check's in the next letter,
Keepin' the tips that belong to the waiter,
Pickin' out tunes on a three chord guitar...
So sometimes I wonder why I get the "musin's,"
With no education to carry me far;

Whatever it is, a curse or a blessin',
I don't sit around a lot cipherin' and guessin',
Chewin' my lip 'bout things as they are;
I just let my fingers do my kind of frettin',
And keep it right here
In my three chord guitar.

The Big 5-0

Fifty is a strange room in a strange town
Awakened in, and no tag on your luggage.
It is looking for yourself in yesterday's mirror,
(What was the color of your hair?)
The features of your face were melting
And you didn't even notice.
There is a feeling of disbelief,
Such as a skydiver must experience
When his chute will not open,
The wrench of regret
Two seconds from the ground.

But you cannot take the jump over.

All those years you cast into the wind,
Loves you jettisoned to keep your dreams airborne,
Have passed you one by one...
In free fall.

Love, Old Love*

I'll gather my memories in pretty bouquets
Wrap satin ribbons round my yesterdays
Take them to market, give them away,
Love, Old Love.
Here's an old raincoat he used to wear,
Stained with the raindrops that dripped from his hair,
Two faded valentines, one empty chair;
Love, Old Love.
Postcards from Bourbon Street
Plane tickets home
Keys to a suite at the Monteleone
One perfect year that we used to own;
Love, Old Love.
High mountain holiday covered with stars
A volume of poetry he knew by heart
Over on Main Street, in some old bazaar–
Love, Old Love.

*Verse put to music

Chapter III

Marriage

~ Part 6 ~

Meanderings of My Mind

Does the soul behind old eyes
Grow dim with passing years?
Or is its shade distilled and clarified
By lifelong tears?
Are keen edges of the mind
Worn smooth by time like rivers over stone
To dull our joy?
Or make us less aware of dying all alone.

Little Bird

Once upon a time there was a little bird that sang from dawn till dark in a tiny garden, all for the love of singing.

So sweet was the song the garden became a gathering place for the townsfolk. Children sat enraptured while mothers brought yarn to knit and spent their mornings listening. Shopkeepers locked up early and ate their lunches under the tree.

All the other birds joined in the singing but the little bird warbled the sweetest and clearest of all. Then one day the owner of the garden said, "I will charge a fee to the people, for is it not my right? I will feed the little bird so she will not fly away."

Soon the bird sang, not for joy, but for the seed. She became lazy and fat. People kept coming to the garden for it was famous now. They came to see and to be seen, to show off their latest frock or hat, and to exchange the latest gossip. They no longer listened.

The little bird grew sad. From depths of her sorrow poured forth a rapturous melody, so exquisite it seemed born from another world. A longing to be free filled her tiny breast to bursting.

The Garden's owner was delighted; the people were listening again. So large were crowds he could not accommodate them, but the sky was all little bird desired. Soon she would be strong, she would learn to fly again, to soar, to sing with joy!

Then came a day she tried her wings. They lifted her, slowly, oh, so feebly at first, then up, up, up! Over the garden wall. She was free!

As she hovered a moment above the sweet smelling flowers, the little cherry tree, people cried, "One more song! Sing for us once more!" And because she loved them she opened her throat in one last burst of beauty. In that instant her heart fluttered and broke.

As she fell to earth the people gasped in surprise. Some could not believe her song would never be heard again. Some demanded their money back. And the owner of the garden kicking dirt on her head in embarrassment, cocked his ear toward other birds–hopefully listening.

Sister of the Muse

She lives in a world as far away
As thought can travel in a day,
A neighbor dropping by for tea
Must navigate the untamed sea
Twixt parlor and the far-off shore
Where gibberish is spoken,
Follow an island's shadow, broken,
Wavering, through pound and roar of her odd imagery.
Meeker souls one league from land
Heave to, where tides reach up the sand,
Shallow and predictable,
Safe in familiar drag and pull of social repartee:
While she, incautious of a friend
Who might go under, dare's windswept shoals of Xanadu.
Lonely again – but free.

Emily Dickinson

Alice-Through-The-Looking-Glass
Your quaint vocabulary,
Since you, thousands new words more
Have swelled the dictionary.
Still, you startle with some truth
Stated with flower or bee,
Synthetic balms and satellites
Alter ways to see
A meadow, or a wrinkled mind,
The worlds antiquity;
But never an old anguish–
Owned by thee–and me.

The First Poet

Into the town he came with quiet surprise,
No one knew his name but in his eyes
Shone uncommon light, and insight rare.
His clothes were old and worn with gentle age,
As folded corners on an old book's yellowed page,
Preserved with tender care.
Neither young nor old, speech undefined,
Yet his very presence soothed the mind
Of those deemed worldly wise,
And children heard the music in his rhymes,
That told of Holy Scriptures lost in time,
With wide and wondering eyes.

Wood Carving

Enigmatic eyes, what do you see?
Gazing from the burl of some dead tree?
Life-like, the old tanned leather look
Of furrowed cheek,
I lean toward those thin, half parted lips
Listening, as if you were about to speak
Some ancient tale
Of buffalo before the white man came.
Even the light from olden campfires gleam
In your eyes.
Though dead these centuries
Some artist here has caught the living dream.

Adopted Out

Pink and blue and silver, soft as down,
Adorned the big shop window in her town,
Fluffy robes, painted bassinets.
Embroidered gowns, baby bottle sets,
Crocheted caps with satin ribbon bows,
Booties shaped to cover tiny toes.
She tried to force her feet and eyes to pass
The wisp of smothered dreams beyond the glass,
But all the woman of her yearned to see
A glimpse of what she knew could never be;
On the crowded walk she stood apart,
Gazed with haunted eyes and breaking heart
Up on that touch of heaven mothers know,
To feel the pain returning like a blow,
For she would never feel her baby rest
Against her empty arms and aching breast.

I Knew You Before

I knew you before in another life,
I will love you again the same;
Though I turn out to be your cousin's wife,
Or somehow we mix up gender and name.

~~~

If your eyes shine out of a stranger's face
When we meet on the street by chance,
We will fade to a long-ago time and place,
To some like circumstance.

~~~

The setting may be a small hotel
Or seats on a London train,
That streak of light, when the world stands still,
For I have loved you again, and again.

~~~

The glance of those eyes will pierce my heart,
As stars pierce a midnight sky,
In a little town on a summer night,
As syllables of goodbye.

~~~

And centuries hence on a haunted shore,
By light of a rising moon;
We shall read our names as part of the lore
Carved in an ancient rune.

The Passing

She hears the kettle sounds in the still room
Bubble and hiss as steam blows in the air.
There is her apron folded on a chair,
Her paper unread, and the idle broom.
No crash of thunder, no portending doom,
A crackle of log is all, and a flair
Of fire to mark the moment unaware,
Subtle as morning glory bloom
Opening outside her kitchen door.
Just in the space of one hand on the clock,
Moving from eight o'two to three past eight,
A soul emerges on another shore,
Remembering pale sunlight on the walk,
A neighbor pausing at her open gate.

Face in the Window

Up North where brittle stars gleam, boys,
Where the world's covered over with snow,
There's ice a foot thick on the stream, boys,
And it's there I'm longin' to go.
Smoke curling up from the chimney,
Light marks the crack round the door,
It shines on her face in the window
And she watches for me as before.
I've been out checking my trapline,
She's cooking coffee and beans,
I'm standing out there on the hill, boys,
Cause I keep going back in my dreams.
Remembering nights by a cracklin' fire,
Cuddled up cozy and warm,
Chinook round the chimney ahowlin'
Her hair falling soft on my arm.
My whole life was wrapped in that cabin,
Best days this old hoss could know,
Peace, and love always wreathin'--
Her face in the cabin window.
What is it makes a man wander?
Something deep-stirring and strange,
Makes a fool trade love pure as gold,
For life worth a handful of change.
I left her, and God knows I'm hating
These nights in this tropical clime,
Heat seems to rot the hard bones of a man,
There's nothing to do with his time.
So fill up my glass once again, boys,
I'm sailing tonight on the tide,
Sweat out my passage way down in some hold,
For there ain't no ocean too wide,

If it heaves up this carcass on tundra,
In land of perpetual snow,
Let me fill these old eyes with a vision–

Her face in the cabin window.

The Promise

Daddy, here in the warm spring light
A mountain bluebird appeared today,
He perched on a blackened fence post preening
His feathers before he flew away.

It started me seeing that lovely thing,
Amid ruins of an old dead town,
Thought transported to a time gone down
When, suddenly in the hush, blue flash of wing.

Transformed in a blinking of an eye;
Desolation, washed in a golden fire,
That gilded rusted barb wire fence,
Crumbled walls, stark pines against the sky.

Between the railroad grade and hill's brown flanks;
Are streets, all nondescript and clumped with weed,
Like little swollen creeks spilling out of their banks,
Sagebrush and nettle in yards long gone to seed.

The hotel falling in and barren lots
Where once a general store and depot stood.
Echoed of olden commerce in my thoughts
And children's laughter from the silent wood.
Over the shamble of what used to be
There blows a fragrance of dewy spring wild flowers,
Above the town, an ancient sentinel
Heavy with rot, the old mine lowers.

Like weathered driftwood its timbers cling
To slag heaps snagged on a river of time,
Tall blue lupine blossoms ring

A meadow, and narrow roads still climb
Toward the sun; and for a moment
I hear it, (or it seemed I heard)
Voices, an ore train on the trestle–
Then I saw the bluebird.

God Star

A star exploded long ago,
Leaving nothing but its light,
Shining down the light years
Into our earth's night.
A ship went out to seek a world,
Searching distant deeps of space
For one hospitable sphere–
And found this place.
In long abandoned temples,
Symbols carved in stone,
Tell of ancient journeys here,
And hint of where the voyagers have gone.
We cipher on such curiosities;
Huge monoliths for centuries unseen,
And maps upon the high Peruvian plane,
Ruins unexplained in secret seas.
Then, a longing we don't recognize
Pulls some inner eye through earth's blue dome,
Up there, amid star-emblazoned skies,
Is our old home.

Calendar

Where blue shadows reached across the white
Of winter pasture to horizon, stood
Mountain and barn etched in sapphire light,
Now old barn wallows in a sea of mud.
Up from the south unnoticed spring comes back,
And branches bare so long against grey sky
Are tatted with lace. Outside my window fly
Early robins, and the quiet track
Through lonely wood is visible to the eye.
Now a delicate green of ditch and fen
Takes me by surprise, and dingy snow
Seeps into lawns, yards are found again
Cluttered and brown. Ice-locked rivers flow
From tributaries swollen by the rain.
Spring takes root in unexpected ways,
For old regrets like winter have an end,
Hope returns, an unexpected friend
Come home, expelling memories greys...
(Reluctant to leave one sorrow hard to die,
...Strikes in the night
As sudden blizzards strike...
Blindingly, out of an April sky).

Far Away

I saw ERIN through your eyes
And shared your love of its stormy sea,
For away from those misty glens
A fragrance of heather drifts over me.
I feel the damp of the mossy tower
Where you watch for a boat that would oar him
home,
Pound of hooves at the midnight hour;
His kiss by moonlight under the bower,
Burns on my lips like salty foam.
Far away, far, far away,
Echoing, echoing down some dawn,
Laden with love his voice bids "stay,"
As you lay in heather centuries gone...
Enchanted I rise from an empty bed,
Catch my reflection in the glass,
Tis the glance of a dark haired lass
Stares back at me from eyes long dead.
I will go wandering in a dream,
Back through ancient Myths of Eire,
Far away, far, far away,
Seeking the arms of my heart's desire.

The Rocky Coast of Selgo

Off the rocky coast of Selgo
Under waves of an inky sea
A ghost, trapped in the cavernous hold,
My love keeps crying after me.
Dragging me down to a sunken ship
Broken apart on the ocean bed,
No way of escaping the icy grave
Of one just a name on the 'List of Dead.'
Of one whose arms were warm and strong
Pressing my body against his own;
I feel the water's awful cold
As I sleep in this haunted room alone.
And neither of us will ever be free
Of his lightless tomb, for he cannot rest.
His eyes shine out of a shadowed face,
As he mouths my name, and my lips are pressed
Forever in a phantom kiss.
I wake with a cry and reach for the lamp.
As dark recedes, "It is only a dream,"
But curls that cling to my gown are damp
And sands on the pillow glimmer and gleam.

Centrifugal Force

Life is a spinning
It holds bodies, dreams, walls of houses together.
Warmth inside taverns, laughter, taste and touch,
Green of day, blue of night,
Whirled in universal blending
Like bright Saturnian rings,
All pain, all joy, flesh and fabric
Compressed in turns of incident
Sailing in ruby light to the top of eyes
Til slowing down of days
Flings off the aging atom from the whole.
In feeble orbit
around experience
we wobble toward
black space
and
fall
away.

Lazulite

The sunrises out of the sea,
Triton rising from his hallowed hall,
Spires turned gold along the shadowed Quay,
Like fresco painted on a palace wall.
One blue spar is shrouded in a mist
As if fog had not quite burned away,
Or just short of the mooring line its list
Had kept the sun from shining on the bay.
Sturdy old sailing ships
Give wide berth her ensign edged in black,
She stands apart among the crowded slips,
Sails forever furled in windless tack.
Poor wretches hunched in a tumbril
See neither ship nor sky,
Or curs half starved along the road
Slink on their bellies by.
The village is eerily silent
Only the wheels are heard
Creaking over the cobblestones,
And the cry of a bird.
Tears on the ulcered faces,
Each interstice of breath
Between agonized cough perceptible,
Faint with the smell of death.
And not a soul to weep them gone,
Deserted the rocky shore,
They shuffle aboard in a tattered pall.
Lazuret, take one more.
No outward sign on the features
Of Disease, or a longing to die,
Only a mind abandoned,

Only a lightless eye.
Old faith mocked and broken,
A spirit in decay–
Stands to with derelict cargo,
Forgotten, and rotting away.

Sea Ghost

The sea, the sea, has buried me,
And at night I dance on the shore,
Listen, listen and you can hear,
My endless singing ringing clear.
You will hear it ever more.

The sea, the sea, has buried me,
And sea foam chills my hands,
You must hasten away with the gull,
I am only here when moons come full,
And I leave no shade on the sands.

England

I want to go to England
It isn't a world away
As it once was,
In this age of super jets
The journey takes little more than a day.
I see the lights of London
But only in a dream,
I wish the width of the ocean
Was less than a mountain stream
That one could step across.
I would stroll the beach at Brighton
Or brave a London fog
With bumbershoot and raincoat,
Have a bit-o-the-grog
In quaint little oh so, British pubs,
Touch a rune of stone;
I want to go to England
But I don't want to go alone.
I want to go to England
With someone I dearly love
To share it all.
On the upper deck of a double-deck bus
We'd laugh at drippy skies above;
Or motor to Northumberland
For a view of Hadrian's Wall,
My grandmother's people came from there
I would see it through happy tears;
I want to go to England
I've been wanting to go for years.

Old World Places

Red tile roofs, white stucco walls
Flank the ancient cobblestones,
Black-eyed women in gaudy shawls
Lean from balconies in the sun;
Weave through long, black shiny braids
Mimosa blossoms wild and sweet,
Scream epithets to frighten the birds,
And dump their garbage into the street.

Vietnam

The silence is almost unbearable.
After the deafening sound of mortar shell exploding,
Smoke has drifted away,
Like any smoke on a warm, still day,
Leaving the sky serene and blue.
But ugly scars on this speck of earth below
Deny the peaceful look of clean endless space;
And pain behind these eyes
Comes from my soul
Sick with smell and feel of war,
The sight of buddies dead
And men I never knew
Lying in blood that once was men.

Christ on your cross!
You are luckier than I,
You died a senseless death as soon as I will,
But you know why–
And I'll die wondering.

Jonestown

There, in the green jungle
Below the wing of our plane,
A clearing, where earth is tilled and brown,
Is permeated with an ugly stain
Of fly-blown human carcasses
Rotting in the sun;
From under cotton dress and khakis,
Putrid fluids run.
Amid the screams of terror, the cacophony
Of shouts, and mothers weeping,
A raging maniacal voice will echo eternally
Through heavy, humid silence all around.
To the impersonal eye of the camera circling above,
Their bodies make a colorful, mosaic pattern
Over the ground.

Tennis Shoes

Maneuvering on tennis courts
Balancing atop fences
Pushing bicycle pedals
Padding down dirt tracks
Wading rocky river bottoms
Kicking cans along gutters
Vaulting over bars–
Shrouding feet of murdered black
Children in Atlanta.

Patriotic Bells

Toll of patriotic bell
O'er the ancient chapel steepled,
O'er the pews no longer peopled,
Echoed down the dell.
Martyrs of embattled home,
In the churchyard dank and hoary,
Time obliterates, and glory
Resurrects ne'r one.

A Story from the Grave

In an old New England churchyard
Leans a stone above a grave
Indented where earth has settled in,
An epitaph once chiseled there,
The ancient date and name,
Obliterated, all but "Caroline."
Suddenly I shiver in the fading autumn light,
While pondering on whom she might have been,
A voice almost inaudible
Is speaking in my mind,
"Listen," and I hear the tale begin...

"The tower clock was striking three
And I was homeward bound.
With dark before and following me
I fair flew o'er the ground.
The trees, which in the heat of noon bestowed
Their friendly shade, where strangers now,
Clutching at my back, each bough
Black fingers on the road.
Half a mile to go
I reach the bridge, and started on,
But Lo!
The little bridge was gone!
Above the waters edge, along the bank,
I saw a bit of rail, a mossy plank,
How could this be? What here in just a day,
Had come to wash our little bridge away?
Still I must cross, must reach the other side;
Slowly through the water lest I fall,
Shrinking from the black, and swirling tide,
(Strange, I could not feel its cold at all).

Up and out and down the lane,
Running now, the gate almost in sight,
A thousand miles it seemed, but home again!
A cozy fire against the chill of night.
At last there was the great oak door and I
Pounded on the panel like a child,
Wanting my own room, a little wild,
Could they not hear? And I began to cry.
When from the window of dear father's room
I saw him lean and peer into the gloom,
"Who is there, who roused me from my bed?"
"Tis I, thy daughter, let me in," I said.
A look of anguish passed across his face,
"What mockery! Get thee from this place!
What heart have thee to speak of one so good,
So pure and sweet, murdered in the wood?"
A dream he dreamed, me thought,
And he'd not quite awake believed it true.
"Please come down," I bade, but he would not,
Only pulled the shutter and withdrew.
So weary now and who would shelter me?
A place to rest, to sleep; then suddenly
There came to mind a little house once seen,
(Or played in long ago)
That stood between
The hill and our hedge row.
Up the garden path, askirt the pond
I seem to float,
No less afraid, yet thought would not respond
To circumstance, the world itself remote.
When from the shadows down the crumbling walk,
Appeared a ragged man with torch held high,
He stared at me, turning white as chalk.
"Ye be dead! Dead and in your grave
A year gone by!"

Now a thing gone raving mad was he,
Stumbling to that little house
With walls to shut me out,
He whirled and blindly flung the torch at me.
I watch as flames spread round the place and o'er,
Consuming all, a blazing funeral pyre,
Licking at each window and door,
At last, as day must follow night, I knew
Whence I would go and ne'er return again;
The thing that must be done was done,
And then–
Turning to the east, I saw the sun.

ETA

If the plane goes down
Unmarked by anonymity or fame,
No plastic wreath shall hang upon my name,
No funereal lipstick on my mouth,
Consumed in the blast, roaring north to south,
Plummeting,
I die as meteors die:
Quick and clean.
White flame across the sky.

Irony

Now, in this tragic hour when good men mourn
Hopeless against unreasonable men who scorn
Our nation, fanatics who will not set free,
Hostages seized, and from their loved ones torn;
It is hard to think their blood and home the same
As one so universally loved, Omar Khayyam,
Whose humble genius enriched both East and West,
Through translation by an Englishman.

Ghost

Two claps of the thunder,
Two raps on the door,
Two eyes ghostly shining,
Two pools on the floor.
One step soft descending
Hopeful, down the stair,
One face, glass reflecting,
Greeting no one there.

Chapter IV

Just for Fun

There once was a lad from Great Falls
Quite expert at doing bird calls
On a ledge he did perch
Tried to fly to the church
Now he's splattered all over the walls.

Current Events

There once was a friend named Khomeini
Whose brain was a little bit teeny,
Assassins he hired
A rifle misfired
And blew off the end of his weenie.

~~~

There once was a queen
So very, very mean
All of her subjects despised her.
So they stomped on her chalice
Burned down her palace
And thus in their small way chastised her.

~~~

There once was a minister's son,
Who loved all the girls just for fun,
When caught in the act
His trousers he lacked
And a poor little lass was undone.

Diet Ditty

Oh, you can't have butter
And you can't have bread
You don't eat the cheese or they send you to bed;
Peanut butter? Well don't even think it,
You can think about booze
But you better not drink it.
Its eggs, eggs, eggs
You can boil 'em, you can poach 'em,
Take the skin from the chickens
And the bones if you roast 'em.
When your legs get shaky
And you look a little pallid,
Just drink a lot of water
And eat an other salad
Cause you waddle when you walk,
Shake the floor when you dance,
You look like a sofa
In your purple stretch pants.
It's a radish or an apple
'Til you go a little ape,
But when they come to get ya'
You will be in great shape.

So You Want to Own a Bar?

Eeny, meeny, miny mo
Catch a fly and let it go
Before you swat it better think;
It up and dies in some guy's drink;
And then the health inspectors come,
Point their fingers, "Listen Chum,
If you are unsanitary
Stupid, lazy, and contrary
We're the pests that you can't beat,
We'll just fine you for the meat."

The Old Pool Hall

The bar is strung with Christmas lights,
Outside the snow is falling.
The poles along Main Street are draped
With banners now unfurling.
Sanding trucks rush to and fro,
Logs are stacked for burning,
Apple cider will be mulled
Upon the men's returning.
We hung a jolly Santa Claus,
The whole gang's caroling,
Snowmobiles are trailered now,
A blizzard wind is blowing.
Old-timers huddled 'round the stove,
Will play a hand or two.
Coffee is hot, beer is cold,
To cheer the regular crew.
Elk have all come down at last,
Tales still flow like wine.
Hunters will be shooting pool
Tomorrow at this time.
For forty winters more or less,
Game-heads on the wall,
Have heard the voices echoing,
Days beyond recall.
"Let's raise a glass to the good times gone."
Bless them! One and all!
And all the good times yet to come
A toast to the old pool hall!

The Barfly

Tonight the old year ends,
And amidst the hats and horns,
The crowd counting the seconds down
To the New Year being born,
She raises a toast to a shadow
As she stands at the bar apart,
And while the band plays on and on
She hums strains of La Vien Rose
Echoing in her heart.
She hears the voices from far away
Out of the decades gone.
The absent friends, long, dead friends
Drinking to Auld Lang Syne
Under a glittering, silver ball;
Through her tears beginning to fall
She sees his dear eyes shine.
Her old resolve to bury regret
To start the new year right,
Is drowned in a glass of cheap red wine.
The neon glow of a Bud Lite sign
Paints dreams, as her thoughts take flight:
"Should old acquaintances be forgot–"
Somewhere in his arms tonight.

Chapter V

Life Goes On

I peruse old paper with old eyes
Legal documents of "this and that,"
Important dates of long ago arrived
Contracts filed away in dusty boxes
Compendium of life's canceled dreams.

Survived By...

It is in death that separates us now,
Not your dream nor mine, but hers and his,
He has fed the earth for two years gone,
A folded flag for me is all there is.

And she now goes the way he struggled down,
A suffering you watch but cannot ease,
Pain, the old familiar, rules your house,
Twists her face, and drops you to your knees.

In some interspace we walked awhile
Side-by-side, I felt your pain and wept,
I understood the guilt, the bitterness,
The passion longed for in that grave like bed–
Where once you slept.

Here I lie alone and watch the moon
Wax and wane, and count the hours lost.
My blood cries out for you, and you in need
Have long for me, but, oh, too dear the cost.

I want to tell you all the things I know,
Hold you in these empty arms and give
Some comforting, a place our tears may fall,
For those who die, for those who still must live.

I am...

Maybe I never existed at all,
Maybe I am an appendage,
A sixth finger, or an extra toe,
A pair of orthopedic shoes.

Crossroads

Once I wrote a song titled,
"Leave me at the crossroads."
Now, at the junction of Highway 32
And Scenic Byway 47
I leave you, every day;
I cannot bear to drive that way,
Though I slow
The car and mark the spot along the row
Of sentinel pine
Just a sidelong glance would catch the shine
Of granite in the sun...
When giant stars dip low above your grave
I seek you out, under a close, black wave
Of glittering night.
I do not stop, I do not enter in,
As though in some desperate way I can
Keep you alive.
Blinded by the afternoon I strive
To hurry past,
If I gaze upon your name
Washed clean by dew
Or early autumn rain
The world shifts, and I have lost you;
You have died... you have died again.

Grief

I turn your memory to the light
Catch in prisms, suns of all you were,
Refracted colors of your hair and eyes,
Your laughter and endearing words that blur
With time; suffuses, flares to life again,
Then dies.

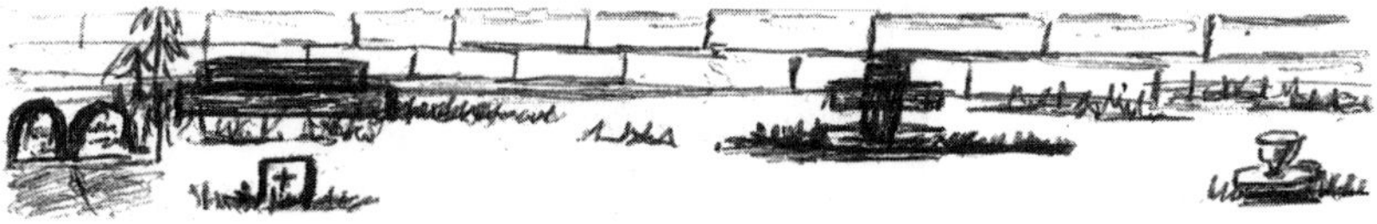

Conversation in a Graveyard

Mist from the river rises, one by one
The dewy mauve of every hill
Turns vermillion in the sun.
Shadows lengthen briefly
Over the quiet street
To purple lawn and sidewalk
Shivering in the morning heat.
The ditch just parallel our road,
Coaxes water in,
It eddies under the footbridge now,
And thirsty field will drink it soon.
Your grave is greening early,
March storms never came,
Snow has been gone a month or more,
And lilacs bloom above your name.
I wish you could see their blossoms
Bursting by the wall,
(Every beautiful thing on earth
You loved, but lilacs most of all).

The world smells sweet in early spring,
The geese are flying home,
Just as they did when you were here,
Just as they have always done.
Could you return across the tide
For only an hour or two,
To see if the sky is gray with rain,
Or blue, if the sky be blue,
Then I could ask how it goes with you
Up there on your distant star,
And know if there is another place
More beautiful where you are.

~~~

There is a presence here.
Not seen but felt, a raising of the hair
Along the arms; a thing not here,
Not there.
A mountain lifting out of sight somewhere–
Hinted at, beyond the shimmering air.
~~~

What's in a Name

Holy water on the brow
Sprinkled with "I Christen Thee"
Engraving on a wedding band,
Time card in a factory,
Signature on bills-of-sale,
Deeds, and mortgaged property;
Forms filed with the IRS,
Check from Social Security,
Chiseled in a marble stone
Underneath the RIP.

I Wanted You to Know

I wanted you to know
How bright and far away
A light can shine
Into darkness of this heart of mine
From yesterday.
I stand here stricken dumb,
Mind gone blank, the right words will not come,
Nor words at all–
Over your grave like scented petals strewn,
The silent moments fall.

This House Will Keep Me Still

The sun shall rise in the East,
The road will climb the hill,
The river winds its way to the sea,
But this house will keep me still.
No one has bolted my door,
Windows unlatch to the sky,
But this house will keep me still
As years go by.
This house is warm and kind
And really of no concern,
But this house will keep me still
Lest you return.
For where would you think to look
If I were enticed away
By rendezvous in some cozy nook,
Or cruise ships in a bay?
And if I am gone in mind
Down a lost and lonely track;
This house will keep me still,
Lest you come back.

Remembrances of You

Before I lose your memory,
Before your features fade,
Before the veil of time drops down
And fills my mind with shade,
Pray, let our love of long ago
Return as brightest noon.
And tender touches in the dark,
Illuminate, as moon
Illuminates the summer hill,
Pray let your eyes obsess me still,
Before the lamps go out at last,
Ere dreams escape across the sill
Of this small room–
Fill the corners up with Past.

Healing

You turn away, so deep is your despair,
From lilacs blooming by the garden wall,
And white syringa bushes flowering where
Leaves fell, a thousand years ago last fall.
You would have nurtured in some other spring,
New life, and gladdened at the robins song,
But this year May is such a hateful thing
To flaunt her beauty though your grief is strong.
All that made your world a lovely place,
Pinched out, as someone snuffs a candle flame;
More beautiful a smile upon that face,
More missed, than any flower the heart can name...
You will awake some midnight without tears,
Aware of moonlight carpeting the floor,
The voice of life singing in your ears,
And love, as you loved, each rose beside your door.

The Empty Book

Fill the empty book
With candlelight and wine,
Roses in a golden bowl,
Soft music as you dine
Turn another page
To arbors where you danced
In scented, moonlit gardens,
And lovers moved entranced.
Omit the dreary truth
Of letters stained with tears,
Instead; each sweet, exotic word
Whispered into fevered ears.
And calendars on walls
With old dates underlined,
Names forgotten long ago,
Flowers sent with cards unsigned.
Delete the paragraph
Of walks in autumn rain,
A face you never can forget,
Of parting and pain.
Fill the empty book,
With life and all you cared about,
(Or nearly all, for who will know
You left a chapter out).

Shadow

She is like a shadow gliding down the wall
As conversation stumbles, and soaring voices fall,
Clinking of the glasses, the "Happy Hour" din
Seems muffled as she passes,
As if a ghost walked in.
A smile once made her eyes shine,
Her jovial repartee
Bounced off the mirrored faces
As sunlight off the bay.
Drinks were raised to toast her,
Friends would gather round;
Good old boys and barflies...
Whispers now abound...
Of eyes so strangely vacant,
A voice so strangely still,
A champagne glass of "bubbly,"
No laughter can refill.
She drinks alone in silence beside an empty chair,
Back in a darkened corner,
And seems so unaware
Of one familiar figure leaning on the bar;
She feels the tug of him, as planet
Orbiting a star...
But he has long forgotten
A world he blessed with light;
And she drifts out unnoticed;
Phantom satellite.

Crying

Serpent stairs trip unwary feet
Colored kites of tangled laundry
Fly in all directions
This foible, this prone to accident
Is cause to laugh
If I were not crying like a child.

March

Snow, snow, snow,
As far as the eye can go
Up and down, left and right
All I can see in the cold dawn light
Is white, white, white.
Winter is winding down
So close in the neighboring town,
But here we are wrapped in fog,
The street is a sinister bog.
It's hard to believe there is such a thing
As lily-pad-pond, or frog, or green,
Or fields where the geese dropped down.

So Too, the Song

I tried to make the most of this mortal piece of clay,
A vessel to hold love in;
Now shards of all I am, or might have been, lie
scattered,
Love has seeped away into the sand.
So, too, the song.
A gift to sing or do with what I could.
All of me that even really mattered
Offered up to life;
No one heard it, no one ever would.
I might have been life's happiest companion;
But – she spurned my gifts and
Turned her head
She is not my friend, the song is dead.
I shan't offer her my gifts again.

The Affair

Just when all thoughts of you it seemed were dead,
Today in modern graphics on my mind,
Was painted, slightly abstract and unkind,
Our last embrace upon your rumpled bed.
Never in after glance could I have read
Your signature, in all that passion find
One hint of cold betrayal; love is blind
To pain renewed when old desire has fled.
A forgery of love that did not last,
The palette smeared with muddy browns and grays,
Held no resemblance to bright colors layed
Boldly on canvas of our yesterdays;
Only the lines were there crudely displayed,
An artist's drawing of a folly past.

All My Loves

I can recite from memory
Like prayers upon a rosary–
All my loves:
Prisms of light through Tiffany glass,
Shadows drifting over the grass,
Beautiful and varying as snowflakes,
Or sunsets on the crest of a wave
Before the wave breaks.
Fingers that pluck the muted strings
Remembered now is silvered wings
Soaring to unknown heights,
Playing my skin like some soft song
Through sweet, long nights.
I can remember June and drifted sand,
The young hand holding my trembling hand;
See in my minds' eye still,
Arms that pull me down beneath the trees,
In an orchard that clings to the hill, and smell
Crushed blossoms under his knees.
Raindrops sliding down amber leaves,
Pipe tobacco and cashmere sleeves
Against my face.
I lie awake. No other trace
Of scars upon the heart;
When did we say goodbye and kiss, and part
For each others sake?
If there is pain in reverie
All my old loves comfort me–
All but one.
I cannot recall his name,
Not one feature of his face can I recall,

Just leaping flame,
Firelight on some long, forgotten wall,
No eyes, no voice to fan the dying ember
Of one love–
It hurts me to remember.

The Fading

Not lacking of attention
A being–noticed–then
In one way or another
Acknowledged–was–of men
Until an odd dimension
Or darkening of glass
Absorbed the light of altars
And let existence pass.

Beyond

When sunset overtakes the tree
Its shadow lengthens up the hill.
Unaccustomed eyes will see
When lamps go dark upon the sill.
Spring forgotten long ago
Will sing full-voice through rock and rill.
Where mist obscures the shore, we know–
There beats an ocean still.

What I Would Give

If I could gaze upon your face
Wrinkled now, as mine,
The dark brown velvet of your eyes
Faded, as a rich old wine;
If you were frail as brittle leaves
In the autumn of our years,
And leaned on me, as I now lean
Upon this cane you carved, my tears
Then would be happy tears.
As it is, I walk alone,
All the hours are but a length
Of broken prayer beads in the hands.
Feat unsure in waning strength
Treat as foe time's harsh demands...
Days are long, and loneliness
Brings a suffering worse than pain.
To feel your fingers curled in mine,
To see you at your work again–
What I would give.
But lacking that; to have you here
However bent your back should be,
However dim your gaze on me–
An answered prayer...
What I would give.

Prayer

By your grace, Lord,
I will survive this daily torture,
This stretching on the rack,
All the fiendish conjurors of Hell
Could not devise so simple and silent an agony.
Free this heart that beats frantically,
Against a velvet cage–
Crying after love.

It Is Over

It is over–
The presence of lover in that velvet room,
The close, warm throbbing of a velvet drum–
Is over.
In a waxen pool
The last drip of candle has grown cold,
A trace of incense lingers
With a scent of old
In scenes once beautiful.
Each heady sip
Of vintage wine is memory on the tongue,
Passion flung across an empty bed,
All kisses wrung
From a drained chalice lifted to the lip.
No light of mood
Can slow the subtle altering of planes,
Velvet lines of youth worn down,
Stiffened in the veins,
Nor fire in the blood–
It is over.

My Life on Paper

I live my life on paper now
A marginary scrawl,
Along these typeset pages
Where memories footnotes fall,
With here or there a name abridged
That held this heart in thrall.
Whispers I no longer hear
Upon the lips of love,
Are specters in the syntax
A poet would reprove
Bound in loose-leaf all my years,
Each an epitaph,
Inscribed up on a blank of white
Where ancient tears have marked the paragraph.
They wait, unbidden, in the dark.
A lexicon of days,
Til dust is all I am, as words
On crumbled scrolls
Old winds have blown away.

My Loss

After I lost the most that could be lost
And part of me was laid in hallowed ground,
And what was left could sit or walk around
Insensible, or from a sleep grief-tossed
Cry out his name; give thanks but curse the cost
Of loving him, the hard years spent alone
There came a passion, gem-like, to the stone
That was my heart, and burned away the frost.
Too soon the hot blood pools in shallow tide;
Swift, too swift, comes cooling of desire;
No matter what bright stars in what bright sky
We love beneath, when love again has died;
Words impearled that only meant goodbye,
Is loss more keen than even graves inspire?

Intruder

Did these breasts betray me?
The soft, white breasts where lover late has lain,
And quickened the blood with tender ministries,
Under eaves, dripping with misty rain?

Has deceit slipped through unguarded gate
To sanctuary, did strong passion breach
This last defense, while inattentive grief
Blinded the heart, sequestered and out of reach?

Were these eyes too bright with happy tears,
Memory too recent free of an ancient pain
To thwart intruder, lifting the rusted latch
Without alarm, stalking these rooms again?

And Later

Bones crying in sleep
Demand a shift in position
Hips war with the spine
Old injuries wage an offensive in the dark
Night is no longer an ally

In Seattle

I feel so sad tonight;
Ghosts and restless flutter
Blind me with their light;
Beckon me to follow–
Would that I were free
Of all the terrestrial shackles–
Dear shades, to fly with thee.

That's All

Peace was all I wanted,
To sit and bide my time,
Not practice chords on my guitar,
Or hunt for words that rhyme;
Or make a tune to sing or sell,
Just watch my waistline go to hell,
Let the door wear out its bell
When someone came to call–
That's all.
I didn't need to take the floor,
I've been there, done that all before,
Being "on" was such a bore
For absent minded me.
An intellectual wannabe
Has never been my cup of tea...
Be he true or be he liar,
A gentle man beside the fire
On cozy nights was my desire;
Quoting pretty poetry,
Holding hands, then tenderly
Loving, loving, loving me...
That's All.

Do You Ever Wonder?

Do you ever wonder, "How will I die?"
Hitting another car head-on
At midnight with a startled cry?
In a hospital bed with tubes in a vein,
While tumors squeeze all thought from your brain?
Fighting in war as, "He died with his boots on."
Or thanking fate for the passing years,
Content at ninety to go without tears
When love has left you ages gone?
If that time comes and what you've done,
Or left undone, has tipped the scale
To feeble steps and failing sight,
And time shows no mercy
For feeling or thought;
Will death seem a friend the heart forgot?
Til you long to go into that "good night;"
Surrounded by loved ones standing there
With flowers and tears around your bed;
"We all love you," the last word said...
In the movie, "All Quiet on the Western Front."
A soldier, under a clear blue sky,
Is shot, just after the cease-fire comes,
Reaching for a butterfly.
Do you ever wonder...

Make of Me

Lie you may in a grassy plot
With a stone and spray of forget-me-not,
By a peddled path in some marked row,
Stating, "Here lies somebody so and so."
All square and trimmed with fence around,
And you there, covered up in the ground.
Make of me when it is over and done,
Ashes on wind blown into the sun
From a mountaintop, drifting through trees,
Or carried by currents on rivers, and these
My resting place.
A fleck, a glint of dust–
Dissolving in space.

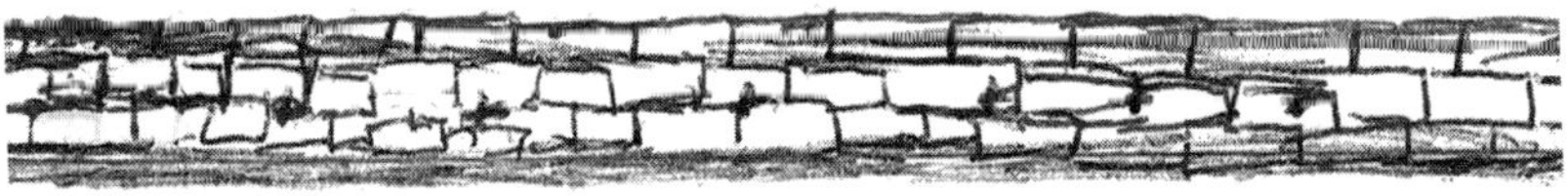

Flash Back

To see oneself at last without the veil
Of old deceptions is a bitter thing,
Delusions keep us sane, and so we cling
To memories we can bear, as Holy Grail.
To deal with truth if truth be too unkind,
Is for the strong in spirit; cowards lie,
Or block it out, the weak perforce deny
The stab of insight...
Let the past stay blind.

No Need of Heaven

I will have no need of Heaven
If gates are locked to me,
If you remember, as I will remember
This night – This lake – This tree.

Stars that fill the spaces up
Around your shadowed hair,
The touch that magnifies like sound
Along the quivering air.

Blossoms smothered in the dark
Beneath your arms and mine,
Though not perfumed in Paradise,
No less divine.

I will have no need of Heaven
Or golden streets above,
If you remember, as I will remember,
This time – This earth – This love.

Order a Book

This Book of Great Poems is an ideal Gift!

Do any of the following:

-Visit our web site: http://www.aspendpublishing.com
-Send an email: aspendpub@fretel.com
-Call: 208-652-3351
-Fill out and mail the form below.

□ Send ___ soft bound copy(ies) of *Sing or Cry* $19.95 each

-Idaho residents, please add 6% sales tax
-Add $2.95 for shipping and handling of one book, then $.50 more for each additional book.
-All books shipped USPS Media Mail.
-Orders shipped within 48 hours.

Payment must accompany orders

My check or money order for $__________ is enclosed, or
Please charge my □ Visa or □ MasterCard
Card #: _________________________ Card ID: ________
Name on card: ___________________ Phone # ____________
Address:
City _____________________ State ____ Zip ___________

Signature ________________________

Autographed □ Yes □ No
If yes, personalized to...